PRAISE FOR
WOVEN TOGETHER

The Fourth Gospel begins, "In the beginning was the Conversation." ...The author invites us to overhear and participate in a conversation which...enriches the Christian experience of being human... The reader cannot interrogate the text, "What is there to know?" without being confronted with the counter challenge, "*Who* wants to know?" At the heart of It all is the call to love and friendship. Good News!

    —Alan Jones, author of *Soul Making: The Desert Way of Spirituality*

Rick Fabian's erudition and passion pull readers into an ongoing conversation that will irreversibly shape the way they approach Scripture and faith. His invitation is the same message Jesus and Paul share: *Here comes God now, ready or not!*

    —Sara Miles, author of *Take this Bread* and *Jesus Freak*

Rick has a thoroughly unique and compelling voice as he shares his broad understanding of human spirituality which ranges from Paul of Tarsus to the Tavistock Institute, from the teaching of the desert fathers and mothers to the human potential movement, from the thinkers gathered around St Gregory of Nyssa in the fourth century to Zen teachers in twenty-first century North America. Rick understands the challenges of faith in our time and gives us a picture of how we might have the abundant life that Jesus promises as our birthright.

—Malcolm Clemens Young, author of *The Invisible Hand in the Wilderness: Economics, Ecology, and God*

Having left organized religion in my twenties and searching for a church that would speak to the beat of my heart, I came across St Gregory of Nyssa and its founder Richard Fabian. I participated in his Jesus and Paul classes, and found them Awe inspiring! ...He offers us a feast, recipes, ingredients, and an open table full of endless interpretations...provoking and empowering each of us to lift our corner and weave our personal thread into the collective human fold...an inspiration and extremely liberating!!

—Afreen Wahab, culinary professor

JESUS AND PAUL WOVEN TOGETHER

RICK FABIAN

To Carl Scovel
from Rick —
with Blessings!
Rick

APOCRYPHILE
PRESS

Apocryphile Press
PO Box 255
Hannacroix, NY 12087
www.apocryphilepress.com

Please join our mailing list at www.apocryphilepress.com/free. We'll keep you up-to-date on all our new releases, and we'll also send you a FREE BOOK. Visit us today!

Illustrations

- p. 3, the author's photograph from his rug collection, by kind permission of Ms Afreen Wahab.
- p. 139, Florence Li Tim Oi, the first Anglican woman ordained Priest. Fresco by Mark Dukes, by permission St Gregory of Nyssa Episcopal Church.
- p. 180, Mars in retrograde: Public Domain by *Wikipedia*.
- p. 187, Zookeeper and Cheetah: Photograph by Richard Stacks, Ó*Baltimore Sun,* by publisher's permission.

CONTENTS

INTRODUCTION

"You have no bucket, sir," the Samaritan
woman answered, "and the well is deep..."
—John 4:11

My earlier work *Signs of Life: Worship for a Just and Loving People* (2019) addressed the questions: What are we doing in Church? and Why do we do it there? Christianity is a corporate movement, and this present book fosters group engagement with two foundational teachers from the first century CE: Jesus of Nazareth and Paul of Tarsus. The Roman state executed them both. I hope to show they shared more than martyrdom.

Three centuries back, armies shed blood over these speakers, and one century back their words still thundered from pulpits. Today alternative messages have become commonplace, however, and as with political pamphlets, readers hunt easy supports for what they already think. Or easy reasons to think no further.

Modern Christian and Jewish scholarship has changed our understanding of how to read our Bibles. Very little endures

unaffected from our grandparents' day, or even our own childhood. Yet common practice has barely changed to match.
Many Church publications repeat Bible passages uncritically,
treating words inserted by loyal partisans as if they were
eyewitness reports. Such uncritical reading makes those who
resisted the gospel sound dimwitted or inhumane, and in so
doing, it renders Jesus' and Paul's martyrdoms absurd.

This book brings modern critical findings into conversation among laypeople, new Christians, and inquirers. We will
hear two provocative Jewish reformers well aware of the
conflict their teaching was bringing. I hope my readers will
discover fresh interest in the Bible, and undertake deeper study
in more books.

In the 1960s, critics began placing Jesus in the context of
his own contemporary Judaism, including ascendant rabbinic
reform, thus deeply revising our knowledge of his teaching,
and so our portrait of him. Today we watch a like revision of
Paul's historical place. At the same time, current philosophers
stress language above speculative theory, while scientists
study cooperation above competition among animal species,
including ours. Those issues center Paul's message on more
than obedience versus free will, which sparked past debates.
Readers will likewise find here new fields of learning, like
depth psychology and social research, which add to our shared
understanding. Accordingly, I offer a non-dualist reading of
Paul's rhetoric, identifying his possible rivals at Rome as
potential friends.

For decades I taught a seasonal class joining those two
ancient voices for new hearers, and for deacons teaching in
parishes. It gained popularity among people who had either
tired of their teenage training or fled from it. One year,
Buddhist teacher Yvonne Rand invited me to bring that class to

San Francisco Zen Center, saying that many young Buddhists would not progress without refreshing their native Christian roots. We assembled a balanced body from Zen Center and my own St Gregory of Nyssa Episcopal Church, expecting a lively ecumenical discussion. Instead, the class membership shifted steadily, as young Buddhists lost interest in biblical talk different from what they had heard in Sunday School, and older founding Zen Center members with deeper life experience increasingly took their place. Thank Heaven, the Zen Center's superb vegetarian cuisine stayed constant. Yet more than the Buddha I have followed skeptical Confucius, who wrote: "If the crowd all love it, you must look into it. If the crowd all hate it, you must look into it."[1]

Like San Francisco's St Gregory Nyssen Church, my editorial scheme fosters lay participation. Members there respond to our Sunday preacher—never debating scripture or doctrine, but offering their own experience. Likewise, my dialog questions here embody a theme peculiar to Jesus' parables: you already know what you need to know. They will engender ongoing group life among discussants: a hopeful gift to church planners.

This book chiefly follows the New Revised Standard Version, among similar publications. My own modified translations appear in italics with explanation in my text.

BRINGING YOUR EXPERIENCE

- *What earlier explorations led you to join this conversation?*
- *What do you hope to discover this time?*

LIFTING UP ONE CORNER
HOW TO ENGAGE WITH THIS BOOK

Today scholars are reading both these first century Jewish divines anew. Paul published his letters first; and yet Jesus taught and died before Paul wrote, and it seems they never read each other. So we will begin tracing Jesus' thought, and then Paul's, to discover where those path lines meet and intersect. We will also notice how their own teachings drew both to martyrdom.

Christian writers habitually reference Greek philosophers whom neither Jesus nor his Jewish circle knew of and Paul echoes but faintly. Instead, we explorers will follow another ancient trailblazer whom many more millions know today. As happened with Jesus and Paul and the Buddha Siddhârtha Gautama, among other early reformers, Confucius' Chinese followers blended customary wisdom into his sayings.[1] For over 2500 years that smooth mix made him a social and political oracle, broadly revered without doubt. Like provocative Jesus and Paul, however, the historical Confucius was a controversial counselor—often regretfully unemployed—and when asked for his teaching method, he drew a homely collaborative metaphor:

舉一隅，
不以三隅反，
則不復也。

"I lift up one rug corner, and unless my listeners pick up the other three corners and bring those back to me, it won't fold."[2] The rich fabric of our human Life stretches too broadly for a single teacher to handle alone, so Confucius' students must work alongside him in the very way that traditional textile artists acquire their craft. That respect for pupils' shared experience aligns with Jesus' characteristic stress on what listeners already know. Yet more, Confucius' own flinty skepticism makes him Jesus' ready ally, from a half millennium beforehand.

Middle Eastern and Asian young women learn their mothers' and grandmothers' skills by weaving a prize carpet together, to store for the youths' weddings. The good news of God's love for our world appears like one great antique bridal carpet woven by many Bible hands and unrolled amid dust and dirt on life's floor. Everyday experience may soil it; and ancient legends and scripture litter it with conflicting religious matter—portraying a vengeful God, for example, which Hebrew scripture's editors actually strove to soak or sweep away. Even where scribes preserved such grim older images out of respect, they overwrote those with their own.

Modern readers must hunt for the fabric's beauty lying there, and dust it off as reformers Jesus and Paul both did. This book lifts up a place where their two different arguments meet like woven edges at one rug corner. Of course each edge runs well on from here, weaving in many more threads. Yet these two teachers shape Christian Faith the way a carpet's long and short edges circumscribe one broad many-colored field. Their differing handiwork even helps mark that meeting corner. Seeing it lifted up, we may recognize the rich imagery woven beyond, and fold it all together to store.

Pakistani Christian Afreen Wahab lifts an antique Pinwheel Kazakh carpet.

Confucius' teaching method suits our task now, as in his day—each member in our exploration group bringing their own life experience and folding new discoveries together. Jesus' and Paul's public likely did much the same. On Sundays at St Gregory Nyssen Episcopal Church in San Francisco, congregants follow our preacher's message by sharing what experience brings to mind, yet never debating beliefs or research.

Nobody will find the same-old-same-old in this volume because Jesus and Paul countered that. But the worth of your group talk will depend only partly on my skill at conveying their thoughts. I ask you, as we go forward, to share your own experience. In my earlier book, ten lay ministers contributed theirs. Here I have done likewise and have offered further questions, all to trigger conversation. Readers may discuss any questions they choose, or none.

BRINGING YOUR CORNER

- *Have you joined a group conversation where you heard something surprising?*
- *Where you contributed in ways that surprised other people?*
- *Have you surprised someone with a gift they never expected?*

HEARING DIFFERENT TUNES AT ONCE

Of course, Jesus and Paul never met. Not even once. Years before Paul quit attacking Jesus' friends and joined them, Jesus was executed using a Persian punishment Rome had imported to shame and scatter rebels. The two founders who shaped Christian religion spoke and wrote different languages, and though barely a handful of years separated them, their teachings seem to speak from different worlds. Paul's letters come to us fully composed, with audible inner reasoning, so that is how we shall read him here. By contrast, Jesus taught publicly for some two years, but we do not know his lecture syllabus. We can only read his reported sayings like beads unstrung and later arranged to bolster evangelists' arguments. For example, lectionary readings assigned to Jesus' trek towards Jerusalem and Golgotha may reveal Mark's or Matthew's shared designs, but do not uncover Jesus' own inward logic, so his storytelling course is lost to us now. Just as the evangelists arranged his sayings for their own agenda, we will likewise order them here from easier images toward those more confrontive. Thus during our study, tension and opposition will sound increasingly strong to us; yet we dare not say Jesus himself increasingly aroused those—we cannot know.

It now appears that both the "Old" and "New" Testaments were compiled during the same historical period, each arranged from earlier books. Our name "Bible" denotes works bound together from documents that gathered materials of different ages. This book will treat both "Testaments" as modern editions do. Diverse readings often appear in the "margins" today, while scholars reconsider which ones are primary. The New Revised Standard Version (NRSV) is currently widely known; and to that I have added a few *italicized* renderings that I judge more precise. We shall observe how words matter!

It is commonplace now to revere Jesus as an exemplar of universal love, but to chafe at Paul's acceptance of societal difference: between women and men, for example. In fact, both teachers challenged the public values of their time, and Paul preached about love articulately, while we lack evidence that Jesus did so. Indeed, Jesus' stories often upheld aggressive exemplars—which many commentators later ignored. Here is one eccentricity where we can imagine Jesus and Paul meeting, as though they might have done.

Love is what every human wants from infancy onward, and none can grow healthy without it. Hence apologists puzzle why the gospel love message won so few converts. Some preachers today equate the good news offered by both Jesus and Paul with *agapê,* a sanitized godly love that shone in fourth century Christian sermons, not long after the Bible was completed. Yet in Hebrew scripture proper, that *ahavah* (Greek homophone *agapê*) is the unreasoning erotic passion that drove Samson tragically into Delilah's arms.[1] Love raises problems as well as joys. Said one famed Russian Orthodox bishop,

"To love is to suffer." (Or as comic Alan King quipped, "Marriage is nature's way of keeping us from fighting with strangers.")

Appeals for human love can engender contest and division, as arguments recorded in the New Testament prove. Church weddings still cherish Paul's hymn to Love and his pleas for peaceful community life.[2] Nonetheless, Paul had a pugnacious temperament that is often overlooked. For example, over circumcising pagan converts, he wisecracked: "So they say...I support circumcision? I'd like to see their own knife slip!"[3] Indeed, Paul alludes characteristically to sports contests more than to philosophical discussions, where medieval and modern commentators feel more at home. His rhetorical quirks can perplex modern readers, yet they show how Paul's personal force might change minds.

HOW BOTH ECHO THE BIBLE

A traditional carpetmaker (male or female) weaves contrasting colors together into rich patterns. Our Bible was written so, and so blends diverse views. Some Christians imagine Jesus and Paul as spiritual contrarians who replaced Jewish ritual piety with a freer humane faith, much as some prophetic critics of worship had anciently done. Yet Hebrew prophets were shrine personnel, and honored the Bible's ritual commands alongside the Levitical priests. Matthew Thiessen argues that Jesus and Paul were both observant Jews, revering rather than rejecting the Mosaic tradition.[1] They wove their fresh carpet designs around the enduring deep field of a more ancient Hebrew Bible revolution, toward universalism.

Hoary Canaanite conquest stories depict YHWH as a handy war god, ready to green-light the massacre of every rival to Israel. One neighboring people are genocidally banned and slaughtered for merely offering compromise.[2] Punished for sparing their conquered leader, Israel's first King Saul loses

YHWH's royal mandate. That passes to David, and the prophet Samuel must finish Saul's gruesome job.

Over the course of two centuries packed with military catastrophes, however, the prophetic and cultic viewpoints shifted together toward seeing YHWH as God of every nation on earth. This shift is clear in the early prophet stories we inherit. First, Elijah massacres the priests of Baal as usual, but later Elisha allows the healed leper convert Naaman to "bow down in the House of Rimmon" if still he must.[3]

By the eighth century BCE, the universalist victory is complete. Amos, our first written prophet, opens by condemning war atrocities by gentile nations—and then in stunning rhetoric, lists Israel's economic injustices in tight parallel. This very *tour de force* likely marks the earliest pure monotheist writing in our Bible.[4] Paul will frame his first century CE letter to the Romans using Amos's identical design, meaning once again: God views Jews and gentiles the same way.[5]

PART ONE
JESUS SPEAKS FOR HIMSELF

"I came to witness for the truth."
—John 18.37

If these words are not Jesus' own, nonetheless they identify his most signal act, which speaks louder than words. Howard Thurman writes: "The religion of Jesus makes the love-ethic central. This was no ordinary achievement.... A twofold demand was made upon him at all times: to love those of the household of Israel who became his enemies because they regarded him as a careless perverter of the truths of God; to love those beyond the household of Israel—the Samaritan, and even the Roman."[1]

Gospel readers have long wondered how Jesus' foes could have condemned him after a lifetime of healing wonders and storytelling. Convinced that Jesus was raised from the dead and alive with them still, the evangelists recounted his ministry to tell worshippers Who We Believe Is Here. On the other hand, their history presents a controversial figure: steadfast in loving action, while his parables scarcely mention that emotion. One touching tale of a man with two beloved sons has indeed been treasured ever since. (See below.) Yet his other sayings focus more on our response toward God than on God's loving address to us. Among the harmonious melodies of Jesus' words and acts, we will listen for dissonant notes that might resonate with martyrdom.

A. CATCHING JESUS' OWN VOICE

As a Princeton graduate student, James Breech once attended W.H. Auden's open poetry reading.[1] The University assigned their biggest auditorium, where students and the public by the hundreds pressed in to hear him. While serving on a national committee to revise the Episcopal Book of Common Prayer, Auden had steadily opposed updating sonorous Elizabethan diction; and at Princeton that day he refused a microphone as well. Soon after he began talking, listeners in the back row asked some a row ahead to repeat him so they could hear. As these made a modest mutter, others in the next rows asked the same favor from those yet closer. Within a few minutes the public could no longer hear his voice among the crowd telling each other what the famed poet was saying. Gospel readers tackle a similar challenge. Far from wishing to adulterate Jesus' message, expositors commenting within our received gospel text can confuse its original sense nevertheless. Unwittingly a few even reverse it.

Two centuries ago, Hebrew Old Testament scholars discovered sources from diverse eras, and so launched the historical criticism which educated readers practice now. In particular, the *form* of a passage suggests its origin and place within ancient worship and life. What we call Form Criticism became a crucial technique, revealing different stages in the evolution of a single text and identifying many faithful preachers within each New Testament book. Form criticism helps distinguish early "authentic" versions of parables which Jesus himself may have authored, but later preachers modified, typically adding material they thought fit well. Of course we may not agree.

Hence the debate over distinguishing Jesus' own voice—a crucial topic for believers—has run on for decades. German, British and North American scholars offered reconstructions that still differ today. This book offers yet one more for you to judge. New Testament critic H Benedict Green remarked, "The more we learn, the more we must admit that Jesus is a man we know very little about."[2] Indeed, each new publication seems to throw fresh darkness on his age. Bible scholars listen for the voices of editors, often very early editors who express their own emerging theology.[3]

BRINGING YOUR CORNER

If someone recommended you join this group conversation, what do you think was on their mind? Had they taken part in such discussion themselves?

New Testament writers cadged details from contemporary literature and local church community life. These afford us little firm biography for Jesus or his first disciples. Even the crucifixion stories, our earliest narrative material, come to us highly edited with Old Testament sermonizing. To show Jesus himself at work, the parables and a few short sayings offer greater promise. In New Testament study, "parable" means a narrative simile that anyone should recognize readily, not a coded moral allegory.

But even there, expert readers differ. Four of our cherished gospels copy each other closely: those attributed to Mark, Matthew, Luke, and the non-canonical Thomas (which many scholars now prize as an outside resource). We call them *synoptic*, meaning they hand one pair of binoculars back and forth, looking at the same source from different angles. Thus, instead of multiple independent witnesses, we often inherit one testimony copied and retold. John's gospel, on the other hand, drawing from a different testimony, talks explicitly and extensively about love, a powerful motive that synoptic parables barely mention.

A half century ago Robert Funk's *Jesus Seminar* gathered critics to authenticate parables from inside and outside Bible texts. Over lunch in 1990, I asked Professor Funk whether he had met surprises. "One," he replied, and explained: for two years they weighed a hundred stories and sayings, slicing open early editors' changes and glosses to recover Jesus' original words. Predictably enough, the shortest and pithiest stories afforded the least room for adulteration. Soon the Seminar decided to publish those parables receiving more than fifty percent of members' votes. Members were surprised to find that only one candidate earned even that modest score: the "Prodigal Son" story (which I call "the Man with Two Sons" in this book), the longest parable of all. Today critics' disagreements spread too broad for mapping secure forest trails, as expert explorers must do. Hence both apologists and skeptics may sidestep critical questions, treating Jesus' career much as we read it in hotel Bibles.

For our exploration, let me nominate here a slate of fifty-five sayings fitting two simple criteria. Some sayings differ from other writing of that time, and so may more likely mark Jesus' own voice. Critics label that a criterion of dissimilarity, which we will use. My second criterion is inner coherence, linking sayings that share a distinctive viewpoint. Describing Jesus' viewpoint is my chief work in Part 1 of this book. The slate of parables I nominate is slender, and my portrait of Jesus may look sketchy. Nonetheless his singular personality arises proud amidst the darkness of what we don't know. I trust your group discussion will assist in this work, the way Confucius' disciples would do.

For a parallel experience, I sailed aboard the *RMS Queen Mary's* penultimate Atlantic crossing in 1965. She steamed faster than torpedoes, and so had carried wartime troops safely. After dark, her upper deck bulkhead hung stayed open, and the wind was so strong you had to lean steeply forward to watch the stars or be blown down the deck. Each night I leaned, upheld by a physical power I felt but could not see. Encountering Jesus' dark shape here feels like that. It is always a thrill to return.

On an issue dividing interpreters, whether to read Jesus as an *eschatological* prophet, such as John Baptist was, I join the party that does *not*. Critics have long questioned the Baptist's connection to Jesus, recently impugning it on textual grounds.[4] Eschatology is nineteenth-century academic jargon for a first-century myth popular with suffering peoples: an anti-historical final act when at last God resets the world aright (Hebrew *tsedaqah)*. Gospel editors shoehorned it into many parabolic sandals as if Jesus had somehow left out mentioning it more directly, and recent worship reformers enshrined it in the novel ritual acclamation that "Christ will come again," although ancient worship did not postpone hope so far off.

Jesus' characteristic dissent from popular apocalyptic prophecies of God's future resounds in Luke's passion story,[5] where one crucified criminal speaks that common human dream of justice at the world's end: "We indeed have been condemned justly, for we are getting what we deserve for our deeds, but this man has done nothing wrong....Jesus, remember me when you come into your kingdom." Jesus counters with his own more urgent chronology: "Truly I tell you, *today* you will be with me in paradise." Luke's evangelist has clearly got Jesus' point.

BRINGING YOUR CORNER

You have heard several candidates for How The World Will End. Have you a favorite? Thermonuclear destruction? Plague? Civil Warfare? Flooded cities? Famine? The return of feudalism? Worldwide illiteracy? Christ arriving just in time? Christ arriving a little too late? All injustice repaid plus interest? A proven unified theory of gravity and quantum mechanics? Harmony with your mother-in-law? Grateful children? Remembering things as they actually happened? Fair rewards for artists' struggles? Armageddon for your personal secret list? Swallowed by a black hole? Your discussion can add more...

New Testament books paint picturesque plans for Ending the World.[6] Instead of choosing among those, however, a growing body of scholars attribute those speculations to other teachers or Bible editors, rather than Jesus.[7] Like such recent commentators, this book will stress Jesus' distinctive focus upon *today*: on God's reign challenging us in what we already know, and on the hour's urgent response. Here comes God now, ready or not! To be sure, some traditional preaching and rituals convey this message also.

B. THE SIGN OF THE WELCOMING TABLE

T he gospels record one overarching complaint against Jesus: his public dining with impure and lawless people, a habit that Jews and Muslims have since honored better than Christian churches have done.[1] For a biblical Sign of his teaching about God's reign come on earth, Jesus took up an image from the prophet Isaiah, who envisioned a banquet where Gods chosen Hebrew people and the unclean heathen would feast together.

A Feast for All People
On this mountain the LORD of hosts will make for all peoples
a feast of rich food, a feast of well-aged wines,
of rich food filled with marrow,
of well-aged wines strained clear.
And he will destroy on this mountain
the shroud that is cast over all peoples,
the sheet that is spread over all nations;
he will swallow up death forever.

Then the Lord Goᴅ will wipe away the tears from all
faces,
and the disgrace of his people he will take away from
all the earth,
for the Loʀᴅ has spoken. —*Isaiah 25:6-8*

Saying #1 • *Welcoming All Banqueters*
Many will come from east and west and will eat with
Abraham and Isaac and Jacob in the kingdom of
heaven. —*Matt 8:11; Lk 13:29*

Like all but one of the Bible's seventeen published prophets,
Jesus worked among his own nation alone, so far as we know.
Yet he dined publicly with notorious unqualified sinners, who
were shunned by other religious reformers: a practice that
many modern scholars think led chiefly to his condemnation
and death.[2] His open table fellowship caused alarm for several
reasons.

For most Jews in his day kosher cooking still lay in the
future; ritual purity applied then to the diners, not to the food.
Roman Palestine abounded in dining fellowships called
chaburoth, each restricted by profession and by degrees of cont-
aminating business with impure gentiles and nonobservant
Jews. So Jesus enacted Isaiah's vision of common banqueting
to seize people's attention urgently. Isaiah envisioned open
love from God to all creatures, across human social
boundaries.[3] The scandalous presence of genuinely wrong
and *unacceptable* people at Jesus' table fit his parables perfectly.
We shall see how his authentic tales feature criminal actors,
premoral children and pushy women. Those criminals are real
criminals: not to be rehabilitated by our "understanding" of

how they grew up oppressed or in dysfunctional families; not to be welcomed in hopes they have changed their ways. In Jesus' parables they never change their ways. Nor did Jesus' meals promise reward for proper repentance. Already they declared that God *has forgiven* all humanity and holds no desire to stay apart from us. Because this scandalous Welcoming Table Sign led to Jesus' death, thereby he laid down his life in love for his friends.[4]

How remarkable, then, that later Jewish usage followed Jesus' example better than his Church did! Rabbis soon shifted their focus from the purity of the diners to the purity of their dinner foods—and the kosher kitchen was born. Today all but the ultraorthodox welcome non-Jews to their tables, while Christian denominations cannot agree to eat their sacred community meal with each other. Instead, these mimic Jesus' opponents, with their various *chaburoth* for diners variously purified. Worse yet, if Jesus' claims to biblical orthodoxy hold —see Saying #35 below—those churches defy the Bible's theology wholesale.

BRINGING YOUR CORNER

- *Have you ever "crashed" a party, arriving uninvited? Were you welcomed or asked to leave?*
- *Have you received Eucharistic communion where you were not officially expected to? Were you encouraged? Did you keep it secret?*

C. OUR VOICES CHIME IN

Jesus' followers circulated his teachings orally for at least one generation before writing them down—and four of our five main writers copied from one another, so we have no independent eyewitnesses to guide us. Typically enough, oral tradition compounds memories together with interpretations handed on alongside.

When lecturing, I lead groups in playing a well-known Telephone game: a chain of participants, each telling the next what they heard from the last. We launch with a gnomic riddle likely by Jesus himself, but now unfamiliar. At each transfer, the player also hands on what they think the current version means. Step by step the saying changes: subtly, by tying in threads we recall from our Bibles, and more drastically, as each explanation influences and reshapes the next version. Afterwards, we track the changes, spotting parallels within our written gospels. Then we examine the original saying. This game exemplifies shared work such as Confucius urged. See instructions in the Appendix for a group of ten or more to play it.

PART TWO
THE ENCOURAGING STORIES

A. ECSTATIC RESPONSE TO GOD

D ebate shades even Jesus' sunniest sayings, which disrupt conventional thought. So we shall study those first. This book will ask in Part 2 how Jesus' Good News led to his death despite love's universal attractions. In Part 8, we will seek Paul's insight into that human tragedy as well as his answer.

Three of Jesus' critically favored sayings show people responding to new opportunity in a joyful ecstasy that renders other desires insignificant.[1]

Saying #2 • The Gleeful Child
Truly I tell you, whoever does not receive the kingdom of God as a little child *does* will never enter it. —*Mk 10:15; Matt 19:13-15; Lk 18:17*

We begin properly with this short parable, which is Jesus' most often repeated, yet warrants careful reading. This is not the

milquetoast Christianity delivered in Sunday School to incul-
cate classroom discipline and conformist citizenship.

Verbs are an oral tradition's most powerful words, and
Mark's use of *receive* echoes a focus in Jesus' teaching: healthy
human aggression. It does not enjoin *being* childlike, but rather
acting as children do when *receiving* a gift.

Even this childless writer has seen what Jesus speaks of. I
once brought a life-size stuffed Yale College bulldog doll to my
goddaughter's second birthday party. Abandoning her Prince-
tonian relatives' educational toys surrounding her, the little
girl threw open her arms at once and seized it. I could have
wanted nothing better. Her action joined love and aggression,
both universal for humans. One motive or the other may dominate a child from moment to moment, but any nursing mother
can attest that the two are inseparable. My prank joined those
emotions of love and aggression the same way.

Recent societal changes make Jesus' parable timely. British
philosopher Simon May proposes that after centuries idealizing romantic desire, our era is re-focusing upon love for children.[2] That love has seen social rehabilitation during the past
century, thanks to a colossal demographic change. Before
French chemist Louis Pasteur discovered germs in 1859, half of
infants, and many of their mothers too, died soon after birth.
Even today some Near Eastern cultures may wait seven years
before naming a child, to avoid casting a shadow over the
memory of a deceased forebear if the child named after them
dies.

Thanks to the relative disempowerment of germs, half the
humans ever born are alive today. And every living person has
been a child. To hear Jesus' parable, we must let go of the
Western Church's dismay at children's behavior. Latin writers
following Augustine accused infants of envy and "original

sin."[3] Lewis Carrol parodied Victorian childrearing in the Red Queen's advice: "Speak harshly to your little boy,/ and beat him when he sneezes./ He only does it to annoy,/ because he knows it teases." But parental advisors now embrace childhood aggression.[4]

Jesus' simple parable challenges hearers to welcome God's reign eagerly as would a child. Further parables raise up less innocent aggressors with approval as well. If aggression is natural, why disparage it?

Instead, Jesus evokes a different aggressive desire that Christian writers must not sidestep: not an illusory longing to *become childlike*, but the widespread adult longing to *have children*. Rabbis, Paul, and medieval theologians consigned that urge to our fleshly nature, which is headed for death. Daphne de Marneffe perceives a similar cataract blinding modern psychiatry. Her book *Maternal Desire* notes that very few psychologists have studied her subject, and cites Karen Horney's protest challenging Sigmund Freud:

"What about motherhood? And the blissful consciousness of bearing new life within oneself? And the ineffable happiness of the increasing expectation of the appearance of this new being? And the joy when it finally makes its appearance, and one holds it for the first time in one's arms? And the deep pleasurable feeling of satisfaction in suckling it and the happiness of the whole period when the infant needs her care?"[5]

Grief counselors report that no pain strikes a parent deeper than a child's death, and couples suddenly bereft of a child too often divorce. That dread experience, repeated through centuries of disease, famine, and warfare, has long inspired meditation on the mystery of a fatherly God's risk when sending his beloved son to face down death's forces,[6] embrace sinners, and guide a wandering world.

BRINGING YOUR CORNER

- *Have you succeeded at calming a noisy or aggressive child?*
- *What have you gladly watched children learn?*
- *Has a child ever told you something you didn't want to hear?*

We note that even the sunny Gleeful Child parable is framed from dark experience: many of Jesus's hearers do not welcome God's reign, and fail to get in. Likewise, two more sayings evoke the cost that adult ecstatics will readily pay.

Saying #3 • The Lost Coin
"What woman having ten silver coins, if she loses one of them, does not light a lamp, sweep the house, and search carefully until she finds it? When she has found it, she calls together her friends and neighbors, saying, 'Rejoice with me, for I have found the coin that I had lost.'" —*Luke 15:8-10*

A traditional bride needed a dowry in order to marry. If parents could not supply that, family friends must, or else women remained single, perhaps as servants. Ancient coinage was dear, so a poor bride sewed her dowry coins into her apron or wedding blanket, and treasured this throughout married life. Mediterranean and Indian fashion now depicts those coins as shiny mica discs or silver-painted cloth.

We can tell that the woman in the second parable is deeply poor, because when she opens her trousseau and spots one coin missing, she sweeps the floor until she finds it. Such a pauper lives on dirt floors, so that swept dust soils everything she has proudly cleaned and ordered in the way her village neighbors expect. And yet upon finding that lost coin, she unabashedly invites those neighbors into her ruined house to celebrate with her.

Saying #4 • The Lost Sheep
What do you think? If a shepherd has a hundred sheep, and one of them has gone astray, does he not leave the ninety-nine on the mountains and go in search of the one that went astray? —*Mt 18:12; Lk 15:3*

The shepherd who runs after one missing sheep is another poor hireling who will pay for such a loss with a beating or his livelihood. Within our text the gospel's editors ask: would you not do the same? Of course, no owner would do so; only terrible poverty could lead you to hazard your whole flock while you chased a single straying animal. We face that shepherd's choice. This parable echoes what Hebrew prophets teach: there is no survival plan outside God's reign. Our choice is practically no choice: embrace the risky truth or die.

BRINGING YOUR CORNER

- *Have you decided to do things that you never thought you would do?*

- *Have those near you changed their minds about you as a result?*
- *Have you told someone something you thought they wouldn't want to hear?*

B. WHAT YOU NEED AND NEEDN'T KNOW

Varying interpreters have classed Jesus as a visionary prophet, or a sacral innovator, or a wisdom teacher. Centuries before him, the ancient wisdom movement had migrated from Egypt and promised to unearth the universe's hidden rules, enabling kings to conquer and their peoples to prosper. Four Old Testament books enshrine that movement.[1] In Jesus' parables, both wisdom and folly do stand out—yet with a significant new difference: Jesus' exemplars succeed or fail without hunting for hidden truth. Even the rules his fools break are no secret revelation, but plain in life. Jesus' fools should already know better.

Chief among common Hebrew religious themes is Blessing *(baruch, barakah)*. At first this word distinguished uncanny good luck, as in wealth beyond reasonable explanation, especially sudden wealth. How God's Providence must favor such people! The Bible's patriarchal legends brim with it; and when later scripture chefs mixed in ethical content for a richer image of God, Blessing still savors of goodness beyond rational calculation.

Jesus' parables evoke amazement wherever God works, a quality we must recognize daily if only we look. Three sayings build upon common wonder at the powerful growth of essential crops for food. (And fewer moderns fathom plant cell division than science journalists may think.)

Saying #5 • A Seed Growing by Itself

The kingdom of God is as if someone would scatter seed on the ground, and would sleep and rise night and day, and the seed would sprout and grow, he does not know how. The earth produces of itself, first the stalk, then the head, then the full grain in the head. But when the grain is ripe, at once he goes in with his sickle, because the harvest has come. —*Mk 4:26-29*

Saying #6 • A Mustard Seed

It is like a mustard seed, which, when sown upon the ground, is the smallest of all the seeds on earth; yet when it is sown it grows up and becomes the greatest of all shrubs, and puts forth large branches, so that the birds of the air can make nests in its shade. —*Mk 4:31-32; Mt 13:31-32*

Saying #7 — The Sower

A sower went out to sow. And as he sowed, some seed fell on the path, and the birds came and ate it up. Other seed fell on rocky ground, where it did not have much soil, and it sprang up quickly, since it had no depth of soil. And when the sun rose, it was scorched; and since it had no root, it withered away. Other seed fell among thorns, and the thorns grew up and choked it, and it yielded no grain. Other seed fell into good soil and brought forth grain, growing up and increasing and yielding thirty and sixty and a hundredfold. —*Mk 4:3-8; Mt 13:3-8; Lk 8:5-8*

Of course, we cannot presume that Jesus told each parable in the same form each time. Some performers rehash routines upon request, but good teachers match their listeners more closely. Still, we expect the retelling to make a parallel point without contradiction.

The first two sayings above evoke nature's wondrous growth power, even in the smallest fields, beyond anything a peasant farmer understands. The third saying adds hazards that every poor farmer knows too well: hungry birds; poor soil; weeds. This familiar obstacle list is meant to enlarge our admiration for God's powerful reign overcoming dangers. Mark's editors introduced another sense to Jesus' gospel message, by identifying each hazard with some resistance their church had met while preaching about Jesus to the unpersuaded.

Gloss on Saying #7 • The Poor Soils
The sower sows the word. These are the ones on the path where the word is sown: when they hear, Satan immediately comes and takes away the word that is sown in them. And these are the ones sown on rocky ground: when they hear the word, they immediately receive it with joy. But they have no root, and endure only for a while; then, when trouble or persecution arises on account of the word, immediately they fall away. And others are those sown among the thorns: these are the ones who hear the word, but the cares of the world, and the lure of wealth, and the desire for other things come in and choke the word, and it yields nothing. And these are the ones sown on the good soil: they hear the word and accept it and bear fruit, thirty

and sixty and a hundredfold. —*Mk 4:14-20; Matt 13:19-23; Lk 8:11-15*

So many mischances captivate our attention, and most church listeners wonder which error marks their own moral flaw. Those dark warnings may be all that congregations remember from the Parable of the Sower. Worse yet, those reverse the parable's import, from an image of God's amazing power into a list of predictable failures. Thus, what was Jesus' Good News becomes their bad news. Even so, Mark's twisted version ends with the same miraculous arithmetic: despite every human hazard, God's harvest comes in at a zillion times the ancient tenfold standard.

BRINGING YOUR CORNER

- *Tell something that happens regularly that you love to see or recall.*
- *Tell something you have watched happen and cannot explain.*
- *Tell something your parents' generation only hoped to see one day.*

The original storyteller (presumably Jesus) means us to share common wonder at natural growth. Pessimists can counter optimists, of course. For example, the speedy unraveling of socialist polities into tyrannies is our past century's chief tragedy. Lenin reportedly said before dying, "We have made a great mistake. What we needed was a thousand St. Francis of Assisi."

Nevertheless, one sure example of God's power springing up in modern history is the abolition of lawful chattel slavery, a reform Paul foreshadowed and Gregory of Nyssa first preached. Prehistoric burials show slavery was as old as the European migration of hominid agriculture 7,000 years ago.[2]

Emancipation rose not smoothly like wheat, but with struggles, martyrdoms, and constant prayer. Abolitionists with simple worship or none at all won nations over, until pre-Napoleonic revolutionaries who had banished it briefly from French territory saw victory everywhere by mid-nineteenth century. Today, outside two South Asian states and Chinese and United States prisons, no government allows slave labor legally. Could recent freedmen or women have predicted such a precipitous outcome from Gregory of Nyssa's sermons fifteen long centuries before?

A like example is same-sex marriage, important for ten percent of folks worldwide—including myself, a married gay priest. That emancipation has also cost struggles and martyrs. Like abolishing slavery, it differs from the morals of biblical times.

Nevertheless, longstanding Protestant Churches—Episcopalians, Lutherans, Congregationalists, Presbyterians, among others—embrace marriage equality now. Meanwhile, public opinion increasingly supports it even in countries where it looked improbable mere decades back. Married gays with beloved children have told me they never believed it would happen in their lifetime. Its growth looks as mysterious as grain.

C. WHEN WE CANNOT KNOW

The following three sayings of Jesus, likely authentic, dismiss fortunetelling in favor of what is already plain. In each, evangelists' modifications are italicized.

Saying #8 • Lightning Strikes Before We Can Stop It
They will say to you, 'Look there!' or 'Look here!' Do not go, do not set off in pursuit. For as the lightning flashes and lights up the sky from one side to the other, so will the Son of Man be in his day. On that day, anyone on the housetop who has belongings in the house must not come down to take them away; and likewise anyone in the field must not turn back... Those who try to make their life secure will lose it, but those who lose their life will keep it. —*Lk 17:23-24, 31-33*

Saying #9 • The Doorkeeper's Lost Job
It is like a man going on a journey, when he leaves home and puts his slaves in charge, each with his work,

and commands the doorkeeper to be on the
watch. Therefore, *keep awake*—for you do not know
when the master of the house will come, in the
evening, or at midnight, or at cockcrow, or at dawn, or
else he may find you asleep when he comes
suddenly. *And what I say to you I say to all: Keep awake.*
—*Mk 13:34-37*

Saying #10 • Jonah's Sign
An evil and adulterous generation asks for a sign, but
no sign will be given to it except the sign of the
prophet Jonah. *[For just as Jonah was three days and three
nights in the belly of the sea monster, so for three days and
three nights the Son of Man will be in the heart of the
earth.]* The people of Nineveh will rise up at the judgment with this generation and condemn it, because
they repented at the proclamation of Jonah, and see,
something greater than Jonah is here! —*Matt 12:39-42;
Lk 11:29-30*

Wise folk seek signs to prepare well ahead for known
danger, like earthquake sensors, tornado sirens, or soldier
scouts on a hill. Within the gospel text, editors have summa-
rized their favorite lesson for our future: watch wakefully! By
contrast, however, these three tough images imply that
enough wakefulness to manage God's reign is not humanly
possible.

Some critics dismiss the saying about Jonah's sign, reckoning that Jesus could not have expected his murder and
resurrection: an interpretation which gospel editors have
added and inserted here. But without reading Jonah's full story
those critics miss the shorter saying's original point. God
called Israel's prophet Jonah to warn hated Assyrian

conquerors, but Jonah shirked his call hoping to watch their ruin instead. Hence his misadventure with sailors and a whale.

Upon his dryland rescue, Jonah reluctantly took up preaching doom as commanded, only to see the whole populace repent at wondrous speed—what Jonah least wanted. Thereupon God explained the merciful outcome: "Am I not to spare a million confused citizens of Nineveh, not to mention so many cattle?"[1]

We will see below how Jesus honored Joel's prophecy that God withdraws punishment whenever wrongdoers change their plans. Poor Jonah had no time to work a prophetic warning sign that might have justly condemned his enemies when they ignored him—a blunder he feared rightly they would not make. Hence "no sign but the Sign of Jonah" means: NO SIGN, because there's NO TIME for that—TIME'S UP! Respond NOW!

BRINGING YOUR CORNER

- *Have you ever missed a plane, or a train, or a bus? More than once?*
- *What factors held you back from arriving when you meant to?*
- *Have you settled and signed your will?*
- *Should you die tonight, who will handle things for you?*

Saying #11 • Casting Out Demons
"If (as you say) it is by God's finger that I cast out

demons, that shows God's reign has come upon you."
—*Matt 12:28; Lk 11:20*

Skeptical historians allow that one fact we do know about
Jesus was his repute for casting out demons. Yet even here, we
have scarcely a hint of his own mind. Exorcism details in the
texts merely replicate other wonderworkers then. Jesus' sole
reported declaration grammatically skirts affirming that
demons exist, in favor of a belief he cared about far more.

As Prophet Jonah knew only too well, God's purpose and
our quick response (or else!) overwhelm warning signs and
wonders.

D. ASTUTE RESPONDERS

Voltaire reckoned that Common Sense must be the most democratically distributed quality on earth, since everyone believes they have enough of it. Some television preachers opine that self-doubt is humanity's chief hindrance, whereas self-esteem should silence our inner judging voice and draw everyone without inhibition. If so, Jesus' opponents were mean calculators who missed his appeal for simple unmeasured love. Unlike television preachers, however, four of Jesus' own parables advocate an astute calculated response to God.

Saying #12 • Pearl Merchant
Again, the kingdom of heaven is like a merchant in
search of fine pearls; on finding one pearl of great
value, he went and sold all that he had and bought it.
—Matt 13:45-46

Saying #13 • Be Ye Approved Moneychangers

The pearl merchant is amazingly lucky to find a great
value at a low price. His ready knowledge tells him to
buy at all costs, even sacrificing all his gathered treasures
to obtain it—and he wins big. The "approved" moneychanger is similar, although modern students may
mistake his identity. Players in the Telephone game (see
above) usually convert "moneychangers" into "moneylenders," a loathed office the Bible never once approves.
Yet the text's passive voice customarily indicates divine
action, rather than official licensing—which the first
century knew naught of. —*Clement of Alexandria, d. 215*

Popular belief labels the very wealthy *baruch,* blessed; and
American civil religion concurs, awarding them social and
political power.[1] Unlike rapacious and loathed moneylenders,
poor moneychangers are limited by marketplace competition
and cannot gain by confiscatory interest, but only exchange
coins for a tiny percentage. They hardly expect riches—until
some traveler requests small change for a foreign coin whose
high value the moneychanger alone recognizes. What rare
luck, proof of divine favor![2]

In fact, something similar happens on the weekly American television program *Antiques Roadshow,* staffed by traveling
expert auctioneers. A humble lady pensioner brings in a
stained painting or chipped pot she bought years back at a
garage sale. She may not recall why she bought art so homely
—but the appraiser tells her this is a national treasure worth a
hundred times what she paid.

The parable symbolically extolls Jesus' own teaching. The
common public may overlook its value, but an astute listener
who takes it up will gain God's proverbial favor. Most importantly, the astute pearl merchant and moneychanger need no

secret divine or priestly revelation. Both use knowledge they have already learned over years.

———

BRINGING YOUR CORNER

- *Tell of a lucky surprise you got.*
- *How did you use it afterward?*
- *Buddhists teach that expectation makes for suffering. Does that match your experience?*

———

Saying #14 • The Barren Tree
A man had a fig tree planted in his vineyard; and he came looking for fruit on it and found none. So he said to the gardener, 'See here! For three years I have come looking for fruit on this fig tree, and still I find none. Cut it down! Why should it be wasting the soil?' He replied, 'Sir, let it alone for one more year, until I dig around it and put manure on it. If it bears fruit next year, well and good; but if not, you can cut it down.
—Lk 13:6-9

By happy contrast here, the gardener knows trees and plants better than the landowner, and he contradicts common sense; luckily the landowner knows to trust his judgment. Both prosper by doing what they already know. All these four astute actors overstep potential pitfalls by canny calculation, deciding quickly against common misjudgment. Jesus' hearers must act likewise, seizing on his truth whatever others may say.

E. CHOOSING YOUR GOAL

Saying #15 • King Going to War
Or what king, going out to wage war against another
king, will not sit down first and consider whether he is
able with ten thousand to oppose the one who comes
against him with twenty thousand? If he cannot, then,
while the other is still far away, he sends a delegation
and asks for the terms of peace. —*Lk 14:31-32*

Saying #16 • Wheat and Darnel
The kingdom of heaven may be compared to someone
who sowed good seed in his field; but while everybody
was asleep, an enemy came and sowed
darnel among the wheat, and then went away. So when
the plants came up and bore grain, then the darnel
appeared as well. And the slaves of the householder
came and said to him, "Master, did you not sow good
seed in your field? Where, then, did these darnel come
from?" He answered, "An enemy has done this." The
slaves said to him, "Then do you want us to go and

gather them?" But he replied, "No; for in gathering the darnel you would uproot the wheat along with them. Let both of them grow together until the harvest; and at harvest time I will tell the reapers, Collect the darnel first and bind them in bundles to be burned, but gather the wheat into my barn." —Mt 13:24–30

Knowing the risks can help outwit enemies just in time. The king going to war runs a major hazard by retreating. He has promised his allies booty, and changing his strategy exposes his lieutenants, who may betray or assassinate him. Yet in a moment he reckons his risks, and now acts boldly. The wheat farmer's urgent challenge is more complex. Darnel is a close relative of edible wheat—but poisonous. There is a great similarity between the two plants until the ear appears. The wind always scatters a few seeds into ordinary wheatfields, where farmers pull up the darnel when they spot it.

But here seeing the two grains thoroughly mixed and growing together, the farmer suspects at once some enemy sower's hand. He does not know whose. But that very trace of malice warns him against his sharecroppers' commonplace reaction, which would destroy both grains—surely his enemy's design. Just quick enough, he orders the two species spared together until harvest, when sorting them at heavy labor cost will yet save most of his crop. Such astute responders must prosper, the parable teaches, while more commonplace planning leads to failure.

Saying #17 — Wise and Foolish Plans
For which of you, intending to build a tower, does not first sit down and estimate the cost, to see whether he has enough to complete it? —Lk 14:28

The heart is where Hebrew scripture locates our planning, and so is the true focus of this parable. A heart's fond desire guarantees nothing. Hence human landscapes display foolish structures never completed, and Jesus' listeners will have seen those. Wiser hearts respond to God now, not later on. With all its risks, this is a realistic plan.

BRINGING YOUR CORNER

- *Did your forebears take risks that you are grateful for?*
- *Are you grateful now for advice you took when younger?*
- *Do your parents look smarter now than they once looked?*
- *Has rearing children changed your assessment?*

PART THREE
THE DISCOMFITING STORIES

A. CUNNING RESPONDERS

Parables we have read so far give only attractive news that anyone might welcome. Not all parable protagonists are harmless citizens, however. A few shrewd responders violate fairness, hallowed customs and public law:

Saying #18 • The Generous Employer
A landowner went out early in the morning to hire laborers for his vineyard. After agreeing with the laborers for the usual daily wage, he sent them into his vineyard. When he went out about nine o'clock, he saw others standing idle in the marketplace; and he said to them, "You also go into the vineyard, and I will pay you whatever is right." So they went. When he went out again about noon and about three o'clock, he did the same. And about five o'clock he went out and found others standing around; and he said to them, "Why are you standing here idle all day?" They said to him, "Because no one has hired us." He said to them, "You also go into the vineyard." When evening came, the

owner of the vineyard said to his manager, 'Call the laborers and give them their pay, beginning with the last and then going to the first." When those hired about five o'clock came, each of them received the usual daily wage. Now when the first came, they thought they would receive more; but each of them also received the usual daily wage. And when they received it, they grumbled against the landowner, saying, "These last worked only one hour, and you have made them equal to us who have borne the burden of the day and the scorching heat." But he replied to one of them, "Friend, I am doing you no wrong; did you not agree with me for the usual daily wage? Take what belongs to you and go; I choose to give to this last the same as I give to you. Am I not allowed to do what I choose with what belongs to me? Or are you envious because I am generous?" —*Matt 20:1-16*

No event presses a farmer harder than the harvest. Both grains and grapes ripen until just before the autumn rains; and while it stands dry ripening in the field without mold, only haste can save it from locusts, blight, foraging animals and thieves. Any who have volunteered for harvest work know the mood of near panic. Like most of Jesus' hearers, this employer is not rich: lacking slaves and tenants that appear in other parables, he must hire day workers, and go early and often to find them; moreover, those finish the harvest in a single day, as no large estate could do. Knowing his straitened means, he responds fully prepared for this anticipated crisis, the way Jesus would have everyone receive God's reign. Hourly he visits the village marketplace to hire more and more workers, promising all a fair wage—even to the least promising stragglers still waiting for hire.

At pay time, the best and longest workers expect extra cash, out of plain fairness. A modern trade union might guarantee their seniority. But the farmer answers that he has paid everybody's contract. As for justice: his limited cash is his to spend however he likes, right?

The workers point to fairness, but their hidden motive is the Bible's original sin: envy, by which Cain slew his brother Abel. (Not the medieval choice of pride.) "Are you envious because I am generous?" Modern psychologists would say that farmer has guessed right. Envy is fear there is not enough reward to assure everyone their fair share.[1] So envious people will attack and even kill a possible rival, even when they've gained as well. Pilate recognizes that Jesus is accused from priestly envy, which grasps lethally for control.[2]

Half the Jesus Seminar voters ratified the next parable as authentic, the highest percentage any parable scored. Commonplace preachers equate the Prodigal Son allegorically with repentant sinners whom Jesus befriends, the father allegorically with our forgiving God, and the Elder Son allegorically with Pharisees who meanly despise them. But slicing allegory away, modern critics focus on the father's challenge instead of the prodigal's folly, and revise all these story characters' ethical roles. To fit with other parables about quick choices, German critic Jeremias relabels this parable as its text begins: the Man with Two Sons.[3] One son's youthful blunders are plain enough; but the father's choices also break settled custom in risky ways.

Saying #19 • Man with Two Sons
(sometimes labeled "the Prodigal Son")

There was a man who had two sons. The younger of them said to his father, "Father, give me the share of the property that will belong to me." So he divided his property between them. A few days later the younger son gathered all he had and travelled to a distant country, and there he squandered his property in dissolute living. When he had spent everything, a severe famine took place throughout that country, and he began to be in need. So he went and hired himself out to one of the citizens of that country, who sent him to his fields to feed the pigs. He would gladly have filled himself with the pods that the pigs were eating; and no one gave him anything. But when he came to himself he said, "How many of my father's hired hands have bread enough and to spare, but here I am dying of hunger! I will get up and go to my father, and I will say to him, 'Father, I have sinned against heaven and before you; I am no longer worthy to be called your son; treat me like one of your hired hands.' " So he set off and went to his father. But while he was still far off, his father saw him and was filled with compassion; he ran and put his arms around him and kissed him. Then the son said to him, "Father, I have sinned against heaven and before you; I am no longer worthy to be called your son." But the father said to his slaves, "Quickly, bring out a robe —the best one—and put it on him; put a ring on his finger and sandals on his feet. And get the fatted calf and kill it, and let us eat and celebrate; for this son of mine was dead and is alive again; he was lost and is found!" And they began to celebrate.

'Now his elder son was in the field; and when he came and approached the house, he heard music and danc-

ing. He called one of the slaves and asked what was
going on. He replied, "Your brother has come, and your
father has killed the fatted calf, because he has got him
back safe and sound." Then he became angry and
refused to go in. His father came out and began to
plead with him. But he answered his father, "Listen!
For all these years I have been working like a slave for
you, and I have never disobeyed your command; yet
you have never given me even a young goat so that I
might celebrate with my friends. But when this son of
yours came back, who has devoured your property with
prostitutes, you killed the fatted calf for him!" Then the
father said to him, "*Dear child,* you are always with me,
and all that is mine is yours. But we had to celebrate
and rejoice, because this brother of yours was dead and
has come to life; he was lost and has been found." —*Lk
15:11-32*

Jewish law and custom assign the elder son twice his
brother's inheritance. For reasons we do not know (blind folly?
bald favoritism?), the father forsakes his duty to teach sons
wisdom and allows his younger son to wreck the family
economy by cashing out early. Thereafter the whole remaining
estate (family, slaves, tenants) must live on near-half rations.
("This son of yours who has devoured *your living* with
whores...")

Sociologists say that if a Mideastern youth today gamed
inheritance law ("I have sinned against heaven and in your
sight"), impoverished his household, and then returned
empty-handed after tending unclean pigs, outraged villagers
would kill him. But the father spies him coming from afar off
and thinks in a flash how to forestall his likely murder. The
father runs to meet him safely outside the village, ignores the

prepared speech broadcasting his son's lethal wastefulness, vests him quickly with misleading tokens of wealthy home-coming (best robe, shoes, rings) and summons the village loudly to the biggest feast he can still afford ("the fatted calf") where well-fed diners will forfeit their claim on his life.

The elder son has lived loyally on bare rations ("You never let me share even a baby goat with my friends"), and he refuses to join his father's assault on customary morals. In a much-misunderstood reply, the father concedes that his elder son—not the younger—is right! Jeremias distinguishes the affec-tionate term *teknon:* "My dear child, you have indeed faithfully stood by me, and everything I still own is yours by law. But feasting befits us because your brother, who was as good as dead on his return, can now live, no longer lost to us." We hear no hint of breaking inheritance laws further, and do not know how the younger son will live afterward. He may hope to hire himself out, but the older brother may not accept.

Yet this father has got what he wants. By cheating on his faithful son's rights and hoodwinking the neighbors just in time, he manipulates the local net of duty and revenge like a Sicilian Mafia capo. Far from symbolizing God's forgiveness, here the father—a former foolish bungler—responds astutely to crisis and opportunity: Act quick, and justice and custom be damned! We can only imagine which among Jesus' hearers liked this story of so many customs broken by all characters save the robbed faithful son, whom Christian preachers may pillory for envy, but his father and Luke's evangel do not.

BRINGING YOUR CORNER

- *Can you hear your parents' voices telling you what is right to do?*
- *Have you taken an unpopular risk that worked, whatever people may say?*
- *Would you hazard another?*
- *Was there a situation where you were not treated fairly? What have you done about it?*

B. EVIL EXAMPLES

For Bible study groups awaiting happier examples of love in action to imitate, worse is yet to come.

Saying #20 • *Hidden Treasure*
The kingdom of heaven is like treasure hidden in a field, which someone found and hid; then in his joy he goes and sells all that he has and buys that field. —*Mt 13:44*

Saying #21 • *Cheating Rent-Collector*
There was a rich man who had a manager, and charges were brought to him that this man was squandering his property. So he summoned him and said to him, "What is this that I hear about you? Give me an accounting of your management, because you cannot be my manager any longer." Then the manager said to himself, "What will I do, now that my master is taking

the position away from me? I am not strong enough to dig, and I am ashamed to beg. I have decided what to do so that, when I am dismissed as manager, people may welcome me into their homes." So, summoning his master's debtors one by one, he asked the first, "How much do you owe my master?" He answered, "A hundred jugs of olive oil." He said to him, "Take your *rental contract*, sit down quickly, and make it fifty." Then he asked another, "And how much do you owe?" He replied, "A hundred containers of wheat." He said to him, 'Take your *rental contract* and make it eighty." And *[Jesus] the Master* commended the dishonest manager because he had acted shrewdly; for the children of this age are more shrewd in dealing with their own generation than are the children of light. —*Lk 16:1-13*

Worse than the quick liberties taken by the generous employer or the man with two sons, the treasure finder and cheating bailiff are scheming frauds. Historians wonder whether these stories retell notorious local events. The sharecropper's plough luckily strikes a buried treasure, and he sacrifices his meager property much the way the lucky pearl merchant does, and conceals and reburies the treasure before buying the land.

By law even today, however, buried treasure belongs to the landowner. So that robbed landowner would win a modern lawsuit, and the thief go to jail. Yet the tone of scandal here suggests he survived to become a rich folk hero: quick-witted, cunning, and lacking only the innocence of aggressive children.

The cheating rent-collector is craftier yet, and all actors in this local scandal collude with him against the law. Leases to illiterates carried a rent sum written by the tenant's own hand and stored in a box where they could be produced to enforce payment. When envious tenants spread rumors of this hated manager's fancy lifestyle, their landlord reckons the man has kept back a rich share which the landowner wants for himself. So he demands the records—unwisely telling the rent-collector he is fired.

After living high for years on embezzlement, that man knows he is too old to survive by tenant-farming, and ashamed to beg help from the ranch's creditors. Instead, he concocts a plan that will oblige even the poorest sharecroppers—who have long envied his income—to house and feed him for life. He returns to each tenant their signed legal pledge and replaces it with a lower rent lease written in their own hand. All tenants will now have reason and means to feed him in turn, whether gratefully or to prevent reprisal. Of course, with an account box full of long-term leases enforceable at barely half-price, the greedy landowner must still pay full taxes and is ruined.

In like manner, your author knows a business start-up whose owner told the finance manager to be gone by Friday. Before leaving office that afternoon, the culprit rebooted his computer and deleted all the accounts receivable. Some debtors agreed to restore their account record for the sake of future dealings, but some would not. Jesus' many outrageous parable characters pressed editors to gloss why Jesus their Master lifted up such a wretched example. "Because the children of darkness are more purposeful toward their fellow cheats than those self-described children of light who yet ignore the news of God's reign." Although some critics misread "the Master" at the story's end as the landowner, that fool and his whole family are bankrupted forever and in no credible position to commend anyone. They belong to the next parable group on folly, below.

BRINGING YOUR CORNER

- *What makes Mafia stories and films so popular?*
- *Have you served on a jury in a criminal case? What did the jury decide?*
- *Has a criminal or ethically compromised person helped you? How did you thank them?*

C. FOOLISH RESPONDERS

L ike that ruined greedy landowner, many of the parables' wrongdoers are fools. The Bible's fools (Hebrew *naval*) are not idiots; indeed, they are smart enough to know better. Yet knowing better, they still bring disaster on themselves and everyone around them. Psalms 14 & 53 warn: *The fool has told himself, God is not here and cannot see my doings, so I can do whatever I will with no consequence.*[1] Swift downfall follows such planning, the psalmist insists, and ruin will spread.

Today such biblical fools fill our highways and pedestrian crossings. Many readers have very nearly met one while driving. Knowing they lurk waiting for us provides scarce protection. Because of their danger, English idiom calls them "*damn* fools." Jesus' damn fools have become proverbial.

Three parables lampoon taking the wrong lesson from the past in hopes of avoiding risk. Perhaps these common-sense images were proverbial in the evangelists' time; nonetheless, they align with Jesus' own distinctive examples of folly, because the unintended result is worse than the original problem.

Saying #22 • Foolish Economy
No one sews a piece of unshrunk cloth on an old cloak; otherwise, the patch pulls away from it, the new from the old, and a worse tear is made. —*Mk 2:21*

Saying #23 • Foolish Economy #2
And no one puts new wine into old wineskins; otherwise, the wine will burst the skins, and the wine is lost, and so are the skins; but one puts new wine into fresh wineskins. —*Mk 2:22*

Saying #24 • Foolish Ploughman
No one who puts a hand to the plough and looks back is fit for God's reign. —*Lk 9:62*

Such a foolish farmer guides his plough animal by looking backward at the furrows already made. The animal will surely wander across those new furrows, wrecking his planned planting. Looking to the future is the only secure way to choose and live.

———

Saying #25 • Leaven
The kingdom of heaven is] like *leaven* that a woman took and *hid* in three measures [fifty pounds] of flour until all of it was leavened. —*Matt 13:33; Lk 13:21*
(emphasized corrections mine)

We will overlook "the Kingdom of Heaven is..."—an opening which editors have habitually attached to many parables— because here the original drama is tragic and cautionary. Jesus' dining with impure folk appalled other religious leaders, who objected that the poor rabble were damn fool lawbreakers.[2] This parable counters with an economic disaster story, which Pollyanna sermons unwittingly overwrite.

Modern translations with "yeast" are outdated. That word originally meant the foam on beer, which medieval Europeans mixed with baking dough to make it rise. The Bible does not mention it. Biblical bakers relied upon leaven—that is, moistened flour pregnant with biological yeast microbes that no cook then understood, but could only reserve from earlier batches, or gather from exposure to humid warm air.

Tasty leaven is still treasured today. Westbound settlers brought San Francisco sourdough starter across the mountains under their horse saddles to keep it alive. Now called "mother," she never enters a commercial sourdough oven; only her offspring fragments do. The homemaker in this parable will learn a hard lesson about that.

For biblical households, leaven was an expensive wonder. Yet each spring at Passover time, to honor the more ancient millet harvest feast, the Mosaic law commanded cooks to throw it out.[3] Of course poor women could not afford that and disobeyed, to strict legalists' dismay. Hoping to outsmart those, one poor housewife outsmarts herself. She hides her precious leaven away among huge bags of flour stored dry for the coming months. (The Greek word *ekrypsen* can only mean "hid," never "mixed" as inexperienced translators substitute, suggesting absurd home economics.)

Alas, she does not understand how live yeast cells will migrate through her stored flour, as they always do in dough before baking. Once Passover Week passes, she opens the cupboard to discover her ruin. All fifty pounds of flour (a poor household's full-year store) have become living leaven and must be cooked quick, as it can no longer be saved dry for the future, and will only rot otherwise. Worse yet, breadmaking requires that she beg dry fresh flour from the very family and neighbors she meant to deceive.

Preachers who would make leaven a happy symbol of the gospel[4] cannot know home baking or that dangerous living treasure any better than did this foolish housewife, or Jesus' damn fool purist foes.

Saying #26 • Entrusted Money
For it is as if a man, going on a journey, summoned his slaves and entrusted his property to them; to one he gave five talent coins, to another two, to another one, to each according to his ability. Then he went away. The one who had received the five talents went off at once and traded with them, and made five more talents. In the same way, the one who had the two talents made two more talents. But the one who had received the one talent went off and dug a hole in the ground and hid his master's money. After a long time the master of those slaves came and settled accounts with them. Then the one who had received the five talents came forward, bringing five more talents, saying, "Master, you handed over to me five talents; see, I have made five more talents." His master said to him, "Well done, good and trustworthy slave; you have been trustworthy in a few things, I will put you in charge of many things; enter into the joy of your master." And the one with the two talents also came

forward, saying, "Master, you handed over to me two
talents; see, I have made two more talents." His master
said to him, "Well done, good and trustworthy slave;
you have been trustworthy in a few things, I will put
you in charge of many things; enter into the joy of your
master." Then the one who had received the one talent
also came forward, saying, "Master, I knew that you
were a harsh man, reaping where you did not sow, and
gathering where you did not scatter seed; so I was
afraid, and I went and hid your talent in the ground.
Here you have what is yours." But his master replied,
"You wicked and lazy slave! You knew, did you, that I
reap where I did not sow, and gather where I did not
scatter? Then you ought to have invested my money
with the bankers, and on my return I would have
received what was my own with interest. So take the
talent from this man, and give it to the one with the ten
talents. —*Matt 25:14-28; Lk 19:12-25*

Despite a common homiletic error, the boss entrusting money
during his absence cannot stand allegorically for God. Twice
the parable tells us—once bluntly reminding his foolish
servant—"You KNEW I was a crop thief," the most hated criminal in peasant agriculture. Jeremias likens him to a Mafia
godfather going on the lam to dodge federal prosecutors. "You
could at least have invested my cash with loan sharks"—the
peasants' second-most-hated rapacious foe. (Contrary to
recent translations, there were no bankers then.) This godfather rewards each henchman as he deserves, taking away from
the "fool" even the money he is still holding. Just so, fools
covering up Jesus' word of God's reign must lose all they try to
protect.

The boss's vile identity—twice insisted upon—undercuts

familiar preaching on this parable. His Entrusted Money, translated into Tudor treasury terms, has re-defined the English word "talent" and advises Christians to husband God's gifts to each.[5] How can the original crop thief's greed replace such fond counsel? No wonder later tellers improved the tale! But Jesus and Paul put a bolder answer: scandal, which we will consider at the end of Part 2.

Unlike the unwary housewife hiding her leaven, this foolish servant has heard all he needs to know. Open-eyed blunders will appear again below, where Paul opens his letter to the Romans. There he argues that pagans and Jews alike have been taught consistently by the law and their conscience, and all know well what God is really like—yet they do not respond with gratitude as they should. So God will deliver them up to punishment fitting their crimes.[6]

BRINGING YOUR CORNER

- *Have you learned something that made no sense at first?*
- *What teachers would you like to thank?*
- *Is there someone you've learned from in this group, and not told them? Be sure to say why.*

D. LESSONS IN SELF-DESTRUCTION

Saying #27 • *Rapacious Rent-Collector*
A king wished to settle accounts with his slaves. When
he began the reckoning, one who owed him ten thousand talents was brought to him; and, as he could not
pay, his lord ordered him to be sold, together with his
wife and children and all his possessions, and payment
to be made So the slave fell on his knees before him,
saying, "Have patience with me, and I will pay you
everything." And out of pity for him, the lord of that
slave released him and forgave him the debt. But that
same slave, as he went out, came upon one of his
fellow-slaves who owed him a hundred denarii; and
seizing him by the throat, he said, "Pay what you owe."
Then his fellow-slave fell down and pleaded with him,
"Have patience with me, and I will pay you." But he
refused; then he went and threw him into prison until
he should pay the debt. When his fellow-slaves saw
what had happened, they were greatly distressed, and
they went and reported to their lord all that had taken

place. Then his lord summoned him and said to him, "You wicked slave! I forgave you all that debt because you pleaded with me. Should you not have had mercy on your fellow-slave, as I had mercy on you?" And in anger his lord handed him over to be tortured until he should pay his entire debt. So my heavenly Father will also do to every one of you, if you do not forgive your brother or sister from your heart." —Matt 18:23-34

Even outside Mafia revenge code (see Parable 25 above), folly reverses good luck so that everybody suffers. A different rent-collector has taken the wrong lesson and will not escape. Excused by a less greedy employer who discovers his embezzlement, and knowing he will be closely watched henceforward, this manager arms himself against audits by collecting small debts that tenant farmers owe him. Sharecropper riot soon spreads across the ranch, outraging the landlord. What a terrible repayment for his leniency! Thereupon his boss sentences the manager to prison torture, knowing that his family will answer his screams by paying up. Thus this rent-collector's refusal to return leniency for leniency impoverishes his whole family as well. Like all biblical fools he should already have known better, needing no higher revelation.

Saying #28 • Rich Farmer
The land of a rich man produced abundantly. And he thought to himself, "What should I do, for I have no place to store my crops?" Then he said, "I will do this: I will pull down my barns and build larger ones, and there I will store all my grain and my goods. And I will

say to my soul, Soul, you have ample goods laid up for
many years; relax, eat, drink, be merry." But God said to
him, "You fool! This very night your life is being
demanded of you. And the things you have prepared,
whose will they be?" *[This is how it will be with whoever
stores up things for themselves but is not rich toward God.]*
—Lk 12:16-21

This egregious rich farmer is explicitly labeled "fool," since his
barn-building plan scatters the very wealth he meant to guard.
A short-sighted miser, he tears down his old barns before
building new ones in order to reuse their stout whole lumber,
which was rare and dear and was Lebanon's core foreign
export. Left exposed for one night his crops might have stayed
safe, as he hopes—but tonight will be his last, contrary to plan,
so robbers will take all.

Despite editors' advice in one added last verse, miserliness
is a mere character flaw. The rich farmer's deeper folly lies in
planning without respecting God's power over all our life, like
the fools in Psalms 14 & 53. Jesus' challenge reaches into every
plan we make—whom we will dine, honor, work and live with,
for example. God plans for all peoples to share in justice and
peace together, as Isaiah envisioned. Clutching our own blessings leads mortals to doom instead.

Saying #29 • Ten Bridesmaids
Ten bridesmaids took their lamps and went to meet the
bridegroom. Five of them were foolish, and five were
wise. When the foolish took their lamps, they took no
oil with them; but the wise took flasks of oil with their
lamps. As the bridegroom delayed, all of them became

drowsy and slept. But at midnight there was a shout, "Look! Here is the bridegroom! Come out to meet him." Then all those bridesmaids got up and trimmed their lamps. The foolish said to the wise, "Give us some of your oil, for our lamps are going out." But the wise replied, "No! there will not be enough for you and for us; you had better go to the dealers and buy some for yourselves." And while they went to buy it, the bride-groom came, and those who were ready went with him into the wedding banquet; and the door was shut. Later the other bridesmaids came also, saying, "Lord, lord, open to us." But he replied, "Truly I tell you, I do not know you." —*Matt 25:1-12*

This parable compares wisdom and folly in youth, where we find them often side by side. As with the Parable of the Sower above, Matthew's editors have redirected attention toward future fulfillment, bidding us wait. By contrast, Jesus' specialty is immediate challenge: decide now while ruin and rescue beckon equally. So, rather than render this as a trite ethical choice between generosity and stinginess, look to a different comparison, as biblical "damn fools" bring disaster to those around them.

These formal wedding customs linger in today's Middle East, where family heritages are as vulnerable as young lovers' feelings. Hence the symbolic ritual of bargaining over the "bride price:" that is, money or farm animals or heirlooms which the groom's family supply to the bridal couple, in return for dowry goods and money which the bride's family supply. Nowadays this formality happens mere hours before the wedding banquet, since dowry and bride price are actually settled weeks ahead in stock shares and real estate.

On wedding day nowadays, the couple's close relatives

gather in nearby rooms at the banquet hotel, drinking tea, smoking and exchanging family news until the groom and his lawyer or friendly companion join the bride's family for a formal proposal and agreement. For both families' honor, this ceremony must appear to take time. An early result would suggest the groom's family disvalued the bride's beauty, kitchen talents, and relations. A long negotiation implies that the bride's worth is high, but the groom's clan so esteem her clan that they scrape for a sacrificial offering.

In Jesus' day family honor and fortune rose and fell by marriage, and that bargaining was for real. The parable bride's attendants are "virgins," that is, her sisters and cousins healthy enough to survive the fifty-percent infant death rate, but too young to secure an advantageous marriage of their own: probably less than twelve years' age. They have brought lamps to light the evening until the groom returns from the required lengthy bargaining ceremony, and the celebrations can begin. But half these little girls foolishly came without extra oil! As the groom lingers in proper negotiation honoring the bride, and as her family support her by holding out for more, all the girls know that dying lamps will shame both clans, so the fools beg their fellows to share.

The other five sisters respond—not with stinginess but with wisdom beyond their years, foreseeing in a flash a likelihood even worse: if all the lamps go out at once, the insult will seem planned, and could even cancel the alliance. Instead the foolish girls are sent out to buy the oil they should have brought along. Moreover, if they re-enter the wedding as a body, guests will guess what happened, and the insult will embarrass both households. So the groom, wise in his turn, bars their entry. Matthew's gospel has the groom using a rabbi's traditional rejection of a blundering student intrusion: "I do not know you."[1]

Five young girls' damn foolhardiness nearly wrecked everyone's wedding feast, until the quick wisdom of five other young girls and the groom saved the day and maybe the marriage itself. As happened with the father with two sons in the earlier tale, quick thinking and action counts more than fairness—an overwhelming urgency typical in Jesus' parables. His story argues that other teachers' errors create similar danger, and our wise response welcoming God's reign must have a like beatific result.

BRINGING YOUR CORNER

- *Have you ever had a narrow escape? Who gets credit for it?*
- *How do parents survive adolescent misbehavior? Dangerous or not?*

E. IMPORTUNITY

Modern readers have asked whether Jesus was a revolutionary. Ancient revolutions boasted brave leaders, and crucifixion became the Roman punishment for their usual failure. Narrating that Jesus was crucified in place of a popular rebel, New Testament editors seem resolved to cancel that role for him.

While all our evangelists give him Israel's traditional kingly titles of "Christ" (anointed) and "Son of God," nevertheless they never portray Jesus accepting the popular dream of a kingly Messiah. Indeed, Mark reports Jesus rejecting it in theological terms: "Get behind me Satan!"[1] John's passion seals the gospels' sole political debate by recalling Jesus' disbelief: "You may say King, but I came to witness for the truth." [2]

Unlike modern revolutionaries, Jesus' teaching upholds longstanding scriptural doctrine. He drew his Sign of the Table Welcoming All from Isaiah's prophecy of eight centuries earlier. And his parables declare that hearers already know all the truth they need, and must respond before it is too late.

For all that, Jesus was a radical, a goad against rival religious leaders, a keeper of foul company, and a model of the upset he preached. His chosen Welcoming Table sign provoked the one convincing charge laid against him.[3] Repeatedly he urged his hearers to be importunate, as he was. Importunity means speaking up at the worst possible time, since success through good manners is out of reach. Creditors are importunate who accost their debtors in the street; reformers are importunate who protest the mighty at public ceremonies. Jesus' parables draw more well-known examples.

Saying #30 • Friend at Midnight

Suppose one of you has a friend, and you go to him at midnight and say to him, "Friend, lend me three loaves of bread; for a friend of mine has arrived, and I have nothing to set before him." And he answers from within, "Do not bother me; the door has already been locked, and my children are with me in bed; I cannot get up and give you anything." I tell you, even though he will not get up and give him anything because he is his friend, at least because of his persistence he will get up and give him whatever he needs. —Lk 11:5-8

Saying #31 • Father and Child

Is there anyone among you who, if your child asks for bread, will give a stone? Or if the child asks for a fish, will give a snake? —Matt 7:9-10; Lk 11:11-12

Saying #32 • Corrupt Judge

In a certain city there was a judge who neither feared God nor had respect for people. In that city there was a widow who kept coming to him and saying, "Grant me justice against my opponent." For a while he refused; but later he said to himself, "Though I have no fear of

God and no respect for anyone, yet because this widow keeps bothering me, I will grant her justice, so that she may not wear me out by continually coming." —*Lk 18:1-5*

Such importunate demands are practically irresistible. At midnight a friend makes a racket, betting rightly that you will leap out of bed and answer the door before your whole household awakes. The child knows from habit that Dad will bring food if he can, and cries until it comes. The corrupt judge ignores a poor widow's plea at first, aware she cannot afford a bribe; but eventually he gives just sentence in order to silence her relentless shouting—even though afterward he must crack down harder than ever on petitioners, to preserve his lucrative repute.

BRINGING YOUR CORNER

- *Have you laughed at yourself?*
- *Have you ever won a battle that was not worth winning?*
- *How can you gain a better outcome next time?*

F. CONTRARIAN SAYINGS—
ICONOCLASM

A number of sayings are too short for Form critics to test and prove them, the way we examine Jesus' parables, yet they challenge commonsense advice much as those parables do.

> *Saying #33* • *Not Burying the Dead*
> Follow me, and let the dead bury their own dead.
> —*Matt 8:22; Lk 9:60*

In Jesus' world, burying dead parents was everyone's most hallowed duty, rich or poor. Failure to bury forebears was sacrilege. Rabbis advised that all other sacred obligations be postponed until this one was complete. Written rules obliged priests to bury found corpses in order to protect passersby from ritual pollution.[1] Even today Jews demand speedy burial, and pray for lost relations at synagogue on Rosh Hashanah, the autumn new year.

New Testament critics Jeremias and Perrin class this saying as Jesus' most radical claim: our response to God's reign supersedes all ethical duties. Luke's gospel rationalizes by adding a missionary priority to preach the gospel. But other accounts conjure no useful purpose, only an ecstasy that drives all else out of mind.

Saying #34 • Violent People Get into the Kingdom
From the days of John the Baptist until now the kingdom of heaven has suffered violence, and the violent take it by force. —*Matt 11:12; Lk 16:16*

Here is a saying countering most other religious teachers. Rather than reprove rule-breakers, Jesus' parables employ them as models. His dinner table notoriously fed reprobates, and he compared those favorably to their moral betters who hesitated to risk their repute by welcoming God's reign.

That is not to say Jesus thought himself a social revolutionary. One of his most famous parables shows the opposite: the Parable of the Pharisee and the Tax Collector, which both "conservative" and "liberal" critics concur Jesus authored. It tells us more about Jesus himself than the gospels' narrative passages do. And though Paul never quotes Jesus, we shall see in Part 7 how this parable supports Paul's argument better than any other.

Saying #35 • Pharisee and Tax Collector
Two men went up to the temple to pray, one a Pharisee and the other a tax collector. The Pharisee, standing by himself, was praying thus, "God, I thank you that I am not like other people: thieves, rogues, adulterers, or

anything like this tax collector. I fast twice a week; I give a tenth of all my income." But the tax collector, standing far off, would not even look up to heaven, but was beating his breast and saying, "God, be merciful to me, a sinner!" I tell you, this man went down to his home *with his life all fixed; the first man did not. —Lk 18:10–14 (emphasized alteration mine)*

Despite common misreading and even some learned commentaries, this parable does not compare a hypocritical Pharisee with a repentant Tax Collector as opposing ethical models competing for our choice. Perhaps unique among the parables, this is a theological story-form comment (*halakah*) on the famed prophecy of Joel, which lays out the Hebrew Scriptures' doctrine of God:

> *Change your plans*
> *Tear your hearts, not your clothes,*
> *and return to YHWH your God.*
> *For God is gracious and compassionate,*
> *slow to anger and rich in steadfast love* (chesed),
> *and relents from inflicting disaster. —*Joel 2:13

Joel's text is commonly mis-heard as an instruction to sorrow over our sins, but Joel means quite the reverse. In Hebrew imagery the heart (*lëv*) is not the seat of our emotions: *Lëv* is where we make *plans*. "Tear your hearts, not your clothes" means: "Quit mourning over your misdeeds and where they've gotten you; instead, change your *plans* and return to YHWH."

Hebrew editors carved a virtual woodblock from the next verse: "YHWH is gracious and merciful, slow to anger, abounding in steadfast love *(chesed)*, and relents from punishing." They stamped it a dozen times around their text, sometimes bluntly overruling the more ancient revanchist theology preserved alongside.[2] This Hebrew editors' theology formed the Bible we receive: therefore this is the true Old Testament doctrine of God.

Jesus' parable says God fixed things for the Tax Collector—just as the biblical *tsedaqah* means: God undoes our enemies and puts us back on top where we belong—whereas the Pharisee went home all unfixed, which is to say, doomed. But not because of his hypocrisy! Hypocrites pretend to virtues they lack; but the Pharisee reports sincerely that he fasts twice a week, and tithes from all he has. Indeed, both his claims exceed the Torah's commands.

By contrast, the Tax Collector guarantees no change of life to claim God's love. Whether he wants to or not, he must continue to add his fee to taxes collected, if only to make his living. "Lord have mercy on me a sinner"—period.

Most radically of all, this story proves the Tax Collector orthodox, while the Pharisee is not. The Tax Collector tells the two truths that Joel and Hebrew scripture's editors teach as essential: (1) he is a sinner; and (2) God has *chesed*—the strong love that sticks with people no matter what. (As in, "You'll always be my child, no matter what you do.")

By contrast, the Pharisee tells two lies which he earnestly if wrongly believes: (1) his virtues make him "not like others" in God's eyes; and (2) God achieved this difference, for which the Pharisee can give thanks. On the contrary, God observes no differences among human beings and has *chesed* for all. The Tax Collector's truth-telling is all God requires to put things right for him. But God will not work with lies, so the Pharisee dooms himself.

The parable of the Pharisee and the Tax Collector represents the core of Old Testament Theology. So if Jesus is its author, he is not likely an illiterate peasant, as some recent historians theorize. This author knows Hebrew scripture more intimately than readers who fail to recognize his theological allusion.

But the parable implies something more. Like the Tax Collector, its author is orthodox, and his puristic opponents are not. He is loyal to biblical tradition, and they are wrong-headed innovators. Some scholars would actually align Jesus' arguments with the Pharisaic renewal movement, though he wears a different uniform stripe than later Judaism would recognize.[3]

Dining with impure and unqualified sinners, Jesus laid his strong claim to biblical orthodoxy. His open and welcoming sign came directly from Hebrew scripture, in the prophecy of Isaiah, unlike the contemporary Jewish practice of *chavurah*—excluding people not of the same group. And it upheld the well-published Old Testament doctrine of God, in contrast with rival leaders of Jesus' own time.

God's love is free. Nowhere in Jesus' teaching does human repentance earn it. The parable's tax collector knows he cannot live without adding his fees to the taxes, and admits he remains a sinner. In a similar Lukan gospel *halakah*, the publicly loathed taxman Zacchaeus learns first of all that Jesus will dine at his house, and only thereupon promises a dramatic profligate giveaway—which everybody must recognize he cannot fulfill. Jesus comes to dine all the same.[4]

It is hard to avoid concluding with Luke's evangelist that Jesus personally liked aggressors and relished their company. At least they were honest and took what Jesus brought. More, they seized the welcome he offered them, as purists did not.

BRINGING YOUR CORNER

- *The noblest leaders have moral flaws. Who are your favorite leaders, flaws and all?*
- *Politics is always mixed. Have you supported someone whose actions you only partly approved?*

G. THE BEATITUDES

Sayings #36–#43 • Matt 5:3-12; Lk 6:20-26

The Bible spells out the Semitic concept *baruch* in patriarchal narratives. It means richness deeper and broader than any rational explanation. While some popular translations render it merely "happy," *baruch* brings richness for all those around as well. This value is distinctly human. Other species, including other great primates, will risk their lives to protect their own young. But self-sacrifice to serve or save unrelated fellows is human, and may help to explain the dominance of *homo sapiens sapiens*—whether for the world's good or ill.

Freud coined the word "empathy" for this trait. A U.S. Navy captain told me that among all his duties through the unpopular Vietnam War, his proudest achievement was to bring his entire ship of sailors home unhurt.[1] The commercial success of *Saving Private Ryan* shows moviegoers share his sentiment.

	Matthew 5:3-12	Jesus' Four (Reconstructed)	Luke 6:20-26
1	Blessed are the Poor in spirit, for theirs is the Reign of heaven.	The Poor have The Blessing.	Blessed are you poor, for yours is the reign of God. But Woe to you that are rich, for you have received your consolation.
2	Blessed are those who Mourn, for they shall be comforted.	The Mourners have The Blessing.	Blessed are you that weep now, for you shall laugh. But Woe to you that laugh now, for you shall mourn and weep.
3	Blessed are the *praüs*, for they shall inherit the earth. [Psalm 37:11, in Greek Septuagint version]		
4	Blessed are those who Hunger and thirst for rightness, for they shall be satisfied.	The Hungry have The Blessing.	Blessed are you that hunger now, for you shall be satisfied. But Woe to you that are full now, for you shall hunger.
5	Blessed are the Merciful, for they shall obtain mercy.		
6	Blessed are the Pure in Heart, for they shall see God.		
7	Blessed are the Peacemakers, for they shall be called Children of God.		
8	Blessed are those who are Persecuted for rightness' sake, for theirs is the kingdom of heaven.	The Persecuted have The Blessing.	
9	Blessed are you when people revile you...falsely on my account.		Blessed are you when people hate you and revile you as evil...on account of me. [51]
	Rejoice and be glad, for so they persecuted the prophets who were before you.		Rejoice: your reward is great, for so their forebears did to the prophets. But Woe to you when all people speak well of you, for so their forebears did to the false prophets.

Luke's gospel records four sayings about *baruch* blessedness, probably from Jesus himself. Like Zen *koans,* these original four challenged common religious assumptions—and indeed civil religion today. For example, the rich Pearl Merchant and lucky Moneychanger share the popular belief that great wealth proves divine favor.

But the first of Jesus' beatitudes rejoins: the poor have the Blessing, because they cannot be misled by good luck into counting God's favor as somehow under their command. Jesus' second beatitude congratulates the hungry for like reason; Jesus' third, those who weep and mourn; Jesus' fourth, those who suffer oppression. All these sufferers will reap surprising benefits as God's reign is now finally beginning.

The evangelists Matthew and Luke amplify Jesus' original four Beatitudes. Luke offers a rational explanation of incalculable *baruch* for his non-Jewish readers, balancing each with a woe against the rich, the well-fed, the merry, the honored. This is a Greek rhetorical technique called *peirazmos,* or turning the tables, warning that all good luck can reverse in time. Matthew, by contrast, adds more blessings, making a sum of thirteen. Instead of threats, Matthew's longer list paints a portrait of Christlike behavior for all humankind to imitate.

H. FLINTY SAYINGS & SAMARITANS

First among those beatitudes Matthew adds (listed third) is "Blessed are the *praüs*." This word means nothing at all like its usual translation: meek. Rather, it describes one who is "steadfast facing opposition or insult, never distracted by one's own anger."[1] *Praüs* is the supreme royal virtue that Persian emperor Darius I boasted of for governing well.[2] In the prophet Isaiah's words, "I have set my face like flint."[3]

Matthew alone puts the word *praüs* in Jesus' mouth elsewhere: "Take up my working yoke and study me, because I am *praüs,* and my *plans are not distracted by narcissistic anger.* My yoke will fit you *smoothly and lighten your workload.*"[4] Joel's prophecy could scarcely want a better one-word summary of God's proven policy. Matthew's gospel summons readers to do as God does, and so inherit the earth.

Saying #44 • *Praüs* in Action
But if anyone strikes you on the right cheek, turn the other also; and if anyone wants to sue you and take

your coat, give your cloak as well; and if anyone forces
you to go one mile, go also the second mile. Give to
everyone who begs from you, and do not refuse anyone
who wants to borrow from you. When you are robbed,
do not demand it returned. —*Lk 6:27-30; Matt 5:39-41*

Far beyond his disquieting parables, Jesus' most radical
sayings extol flinty behavior such as Isaiah and Darius I
praised. These contrarian counsels are virtues for disciplined
leaders, not oppressed underdogs.

The Beatitudes' disruptive tone affirms Jesus' authorship.
The passion stories reveal Jesus as truth's royal hero, staunchly
strong (*chesed*) in contrast to pliant Pilate, forthright (*yashar*)
in contrast to conniving priests, steady (*emeth*) in contrast to
the fickle mob, and resolute (*praüs*) in contrast to his own
fleeing friends.

Jesus' radical flinty sayings do not even mention revenge or
retribution, which might distract an authoritative ruler from
his sworn purpose.[5] Muslims rank Jesus among the five *Posses-
sors of Steadfastness ('Ul al-Asm),* and teach that Jesus always
speaks the Truth.[6]

BRINGING YOUR CORNER

- *Have you experienced steadfast endurance? Was it
  hard?*
- *What moral accounts remain to be balanced before
  Justice reigns?*
- *What if they will not balance?*

In whatever ways riches empower our daily living, they also distract us from honoring God's reign over all life, as God made us to do. Even our bodily purity, though enjoined in scripture, can disguise the truth that moral power belongs to God alone. The next four dramatic sayings warn that even while riches and ritual purity may evidence God's blessing (*baruch*), they also can accompany ethical failure.

Saying #45 • Camel & Needle
It is easier for a camel to go through the eye of a needle than for someone who is rich to enter the kingdom of God. —*Mk 10:25; Matt 19:24; Lk 18:24*

Saying #45 • Nothing Outside Defiles
There is nothing outside a person that by going in can defile, but the things that come out are what defile. —Mk *7:15; Matt 15:17*

Like the Beatitudes, these two possible proverbs rebut popular superstition rather than formal teaching. Thiessen argues that Jesus and Paul were both observant Jews who personally honored Mosaic ritual commands as well as moral commands. (Indeed, several other rabbis stressed ritual's inward spiritual sense.)[7] For example, the debate about Sabbath healings in Matthew 12 retails a likely Christian canard, whereas in fact other sources show contemporary rabbis advocating Sabbath day kindnesses. Nonetheless, two singular sayings in Jesus' voice blunt iconoclasm.

Saying #46 • Dragnet
Again, the kingdom of heaven is like a net that was thrown into the sea and caught fish of every kind; when it was full, they drew it ashore, sat down, and put the

good into baskets but threw out the bad. —*Matt 13:47-48*

Supremely destructive among fishing tools, a dragnet kills all fish, good and bad alike. The bad fish are thrown away into the sea or sand while the good are eaten. None survive, let alone reproduce. (A happier implication for the good fish proves Matthew's editor is no fisherman.) So much for popular dreams of an apocalyptic *tsedaqah,* when God would replace our corrupt world order, set Israel back atop the nations where she belongs, and reverse injustices the righteous have suffered! As the prophet Amos warns, that "Day of the Lord" will be a day of darkness, not of light.[8] All humans have the same value in God's eyes—contrary to the two great lies that Luke's Pharisee sincerely believes—and God's reign judges us all.

Some gospel critics dismiss the short dragnet simile, pleading that a Last Judgment was dear to later New Testament writers, but not to Jesus himself. Yet if we read it closely, this parable actually overrules popular Last Judgment hopes, and echoes ancient prophets like Amos, as Jesus often did.

Saying #47 • Good Samaritan

A man was going down from Jerusalem to Jericho, and fell into the hands of robbers, who stripped him, beat him, and went away, leaving him half dead. Now by chance a priest was going down that road; and when he had *eyed* him, he passed by on the other side. So likewise a Levite, when he came to the place and *eyed* him, passed by on the other side. But a Samaritan while traveling came near him; and when he *glimpsed* him, he was moved with pity. He went to him and bandaged his wounds, having poured oil and wine on them. Then he put him on his own animal, brought him to an inn, and

took care of him. The next day he took out two denarii,
gave them to the innkeeper, and said, "Take care of
him; and when I come back, I will repay you whatever
more you spend." Which of these three, do you think,
was a neighbor to the man who fell into the hands of
the robbers? —*Lk 10:29-36*

For this story's protagonist, Jesus invents not the ordinary
layman whom listeners might expect, but a Samaritan. Nor is
he a historical hero whose inner conflicts we might evaluate
(for example, the way reading Napoleon's letters shapes judgment of his dictatorship). This man is folk fiction and stands
for a popular schism in Jesus' day.

Samaritans were believers who still kept older Jewish
rituals at local shrines, which priests and royal reformers had
suppressed in favor of one Jerusalem temple, where ritual
could be supervised to evade God's anger.[9] Samaritans' resent-
ment against that reform generated aggressive violence.
During Jesus' lifetime they stole into the Jerusalem temple
court at midnight during Passover, scattering human bones so
that no pious Jew could keep the festival there that year.[10]

"Neighbor" then meant a fellow-Jew and heir to Abraham,
though of another tribe: the Samaritan dissidents were just
such neighbors. A priest and Levite, both upstanding
Jerusalem temple staff members, eye the robbery victim as
good men naturally might, hoping for signs of life and so a
plain chance to help him.[11] But the robbers had left him for
dead in order to escape identification and arraignment later,[12]
so the victim shows no such vital signs.

Thiessen explains that the priests' conflict lies not between
a scrupulous ritual standard and a humane call for kindness,
but between two priestly rules: one commands a priest to bury
a corpse found anywhere, while another commands him to

avoid pollution by a corpse.[13] Rabbis argued then over which duty must prevail. Here Jesus joins the rabbis' debate without downgrading ritual purity itself.

Importantly, the Samaritan responds at once, while the others dither and retire. Jesus' bold hero resents the Temple's rule and takes up the victim, who could very well die in his arms and ruin his own ritual purity. After describing the Samaritan heretic's *generosity* and *faithfulness*, the story ends with his *promise* to pay innkeeper's costs. Those three words name most rabbis' top ethical ideals: God is *generous*, and *faithful* Jews inherit God's *promise*, which grounds their national existence. The cowardly priest and Levite betray all three.

Rather than opposing humane kindness against ritual scruple, this parable extolls compassionate generosity and urgent response—recurrent themes for Jesus. And yet these virtues make this his most iconoclastic story. He chooses as its hero not just another cunning opportunist or criminal, but a dissident, who shames the lofty agents of mainline religious reform (possibly Jesus' own party) by his threefold biblical virtue.

The Hebrew prophets offered a similar rebuke. Amos might have had God say, "Worshippers, you could please me by adding in a little justice along with the rituals." But instead he promises,

> Even though you offer me your burnt-offerings and
> grain-offerings,
> I will not accept them;
> and the offerings of well-being of your fatted animals
> I will not look upon. —*Amos 5:22*

It would be hard to frame stronger iconoclasm than that.

For our New Testament woven tapestry, the Samaritan schism may have bequeathed us grander stuff yet. Leading commentator Raymond Brown proposes that John's gospel and three Johannine letters come from a Samaritan Christian community struggling in vain against a riptide of gnostic myths, which finally drowned their theology by century's end.[14] Samaritan Jews maintain their separate rabbis and rituals in Israel to this day.

BRINGING YOUR CORNER

- *What other religious traditions do you know personally?*
- *Nowadays people of other faiths heal our sick, teach our children, clean our homes, and safeguard our streets. What gifts do people of other faiths offer to contemporary Christians?*
- *What should Christians teach their own children about other faiths?*

PART FOUR
JESUS SPEAKS AMONG FRIENDS

Whoever is not against us is for us.
—Mark 9:40

In biblical criticism, the criterion of dissimilarity helps us to distinguish which words show Jesus' telltale voice. Thus, if a saying attributed to Jesus differs from those of contemporary Jewish teachers or even a gospel's author, it is likely authentic. But Jesus did not say odd things only. Recent scholarship finds that his dialogues honored Levitical commands, and so fit among other contemporary rabbinical reforms.[1] Furthermore, our gospel texts link Jesus with the Bible's prophets in particular. His failure to gather a strong following and his mob punishment fit prophetic tradition, as the evangelists repeatedly point out.

We often hear Jesus' own words blended with others' words. Many creative traditions have conveyed mixtures deliberately. Renaissance composers such as Dufay and Brumel wove popular ditties they expected worshippers to recognize into their monumental masses. J.S. Bach's closed his Goldberg Variations with a medley of village children's songs.

Second century evangelists did something similar. The gospel writers attribute to Jesus alone treasured parables and sayings that exhibit composites of multiple authors. Some attributions are partly plausible, some likely proverbial. Yet without getting bogged down in exhaustive analysis, we can hope to catch Jesus' distinctive voice among the choir.

A. THE CORONA IN OUR DARK SKY: GOD'S LOVE FOR THE POOR

Twelve times yearly a revolving moon passes between our Earth and our Sun. Each month the moon's shadow courses differently across our spinning planet. That shadow seen from its center can reveal a wonder like none other. Eclipses fascinate human viewers as we watch our heavenly lights shift power briefly. But a total solar eclipse is different. For six minutes the darkened moon overhead exposes the sun's corona, a vast lace of energy branching into the sky like the veins in a human eye.

Earthbound humans never perceive the sun's energy crown any other way. This writer watched a full solar eclipse in Oregon. Photographs had scarcely prepared me: it was like staring into the eye of God, veins and all. No wonder some become addicted and travel expensively to exotic, dangerous places in order to glimpse it again and again. The experience transforms humdrum life. I hope to witness it once more before my death.

Reading Jesus' published words reveals God's eye in just such a way. Text critics may point to singular sayings that no one else would have created, like our lunar disc, while their energy traces farther back into timeless space. Indeed, Jesus' own reverence for Hebrew prophets anchors him within a tradition joined by many more teachers.

One bold theme from the prophets, chorused in his day as in ours, is that God watches specially over the poor. No wonder among all the commonplace melodies woven into the gospel, this tune resonates in Jesus' voice. Stanford University primatologist Robert Sapolsky writes that many animal species share talents formerly thought a select human province: tools, language, music, arithmetic, monogamy, justice, revenge, forgiveness, and more.[1] Human primates boast only one unique social phenomenon that no other species has —poverty.

Prehistoric burial sites show that difference already. And no historical political structure has successfully closed humanity's growing wealth gap. Our poor include other animal species too, which we can care for or destroy. Under human management their worldwide array dwindles terribly today.

BRINGING YOUR CORNER

- *What charities do you support? Are they all Church charities?*
- *Your neighboring Muslims and Jews preach charity constantly. Have you learned what they do?*
- *Do you budget for it? How about in your will?*

Jesus' chosen welcoming sign of dining with tax collectors and harlots placed him in lowly company habitually. Inspired by Isaiah's vision of a banquet for all peoples, his behavior matched his parable characters drawn from social underlings, and aroused disparaging insults from ascendant purist reformers. His storied advice to a rich young ruler—"Go sell all you have and give to the poor and come follow me"—may be legendary, but it implies that so wealthy a hearer was uncommon among his friends.[2] One day those very words would move wealthy Francis of Assisi to follow Jesus by a life that even Lenin revered.

For good reason, then, gospel poverty tales often include a banquet and a surprise. If some sayings stitched into our gospel texts were not from Jesus, a few fit close enough for evangelists to weave them in. Jesus' distinctive emphasis that people already know all they need to know blends well into that cloth.

B. SPOILING YOUR SUPPER

Saying #48 • *Great Supper*

An *oligarch* gave a great wedding dinner and invited many. At the time for the dinner he sent his slave to say to those who had been invited, "Come; for everything is ready now." But they all alike began to make excuses. The first said to him, "I have bought a piece of land, and I must go out and see it; please accept my regrets." Another said, "I have bought five yoke of oxen, and I am going to try them out; please accept my regrets." Another said, "I have just been married, and therefore I cannot come." So the slave returned and reported this to his master. Then the owner of the house became angry and said to his slave, "Go out at once into the streets and lanes of the town and bring in the poor, the crippled, the blind, and the lame." And the slave said, "Sir, what you ordered has been done, and there is still room." Then the master said to the slave, "Go out into the roads and *field-edge* lanes, and compel people to come in, so that my house may be filled. For I tell you,

none of those who were invited will taste my dinner."
—*Matt 22.1-10*

Saying #49 • Man Without a Wedding Robe
But when the *oligarch* came in to see the guests, he
noticed a man there who was not wearing a wedding
robe, and he said to him, "Friend, how did you get in
here without a wedding robe?" And *the man* was
speechless. Then the *oligarch* said to the attendants,
"Bind him hand and foot, and throw him out into *the
dark cold*, where there will be *moaning and chattering*
teeth." —*Matt 22:11-14*

Rich Middle Eastern hosts invited their solemn festal
guests weeks ahead, and sent servants to bring them
safely at the appointed hour. The parade of
elegantly festooned guests escorted through dangerous streets
to the banquet, some on palanquins, drew public admiration
and envy. See how these are honored above the rest of us! The
host normally dined apart, but circulated among his guests as
they banqueted, receiving their thanks, compliments and
blessings.

Against this grandiose hospitality pattern, two parables
depict a lavish wedding banquet gone wrong, embarrassing
everyone. Repeatedly the servants arriving to gather guests
from their houses find them absent, or inventing excuses to
avoid public connection with their social-climbing host. One
guest blames his own marital obligations. A second pleads
urgent farming business with expensive new draught animals.
In a third case those servants find a guest improperly dressed:
evidently he had planned to dodge the event, but lingered too
long before vanishing. Parading this scruffy socialite through
the streets would expose his low opinion of the marriage

alliance, for the whole city to laugh at its pretension. He hopes an embarrassed host will let him hide away.

On the contrary, the mortified *oligarch* strikes back at once. Out with the shaming shabby dresser! And in place of social luminaries, the palanquins will round up street beggars, bearing those aloft past the invited guests' gates for the public to laugh—only now at the devious snobs who are no longer welcome. If the banquet hall still has space, the servants shall corral the starving migrants from highways, and the harvest-scavengers from field borders, driving them in uncivilly like farm animals to feed. This way the host will hardly gild his social standing, but he will eat sweet revenge served cold, as the Spanish proverb puts it.

Thus if only for the meanest reasons, the extreme poor are cared for and enjoy God's blessing by sudden surprise, without anyone designing ahead. Such sudden benefit sparks several of Jesus' authentic stories. God's arresting love surpasses reason and demands our readiness to welcome it—or miss our life-time chance otherwise.

C. BAR MAAJAN AND
LAZARUS

Scholars have uncovered an Alexandrian original behind one more tale, featuring a rich tax farmer Bar Maajan in Hell, as commonly expected. And yet Bar Maajan's script echoes Jesus' storied surprises, although Jesus' own parables never warn of a lingering posthumous doom but rather a speedy undoing.[1]

Saying #50 • Six Brothers
There was a rich man who was dressed in purple and fine linen and who feasted sumptuously every day. And at his gate lay a poor man named Lazarus, covered with sores, who longed to satisfy his hunger with what fell from the rich man's table; even the dogs would come and lick his sores. The poor man died and was carried away by the angels to be with Abraham. The rich man also died and was buried. In Hades, where he was being tormented, he looked up and saw Abraham far away with Lazarus by his side. He called out, "Father Abra-

ham, have mercy on me, and send Lazarus to dip the tip of his finger in water and cool my tongue; for I am in agony in these flames." But Abraham said, "Child, remember that during your lifetime you received your good things, and Lazarus in like manner evil things; but now he is comforted here, and you are in agony. Besides all this, between you and us a great chasm has been fixed, so that those who might want to pass from here to you cannot do so, and no one can cross from there to us." He said, "Then, father, I beg you to send him to my father's house—for I have five brothers— that he may warn them, so that they will not also come into this place of torment." Abraham replied, "They have Moses and the prophets; they should listen to them." He said, "No, father Abraham; but if someone goes to them from the dead, they will repent." He said to him, "If they do not listen to Moses and the prophets, neither will they be convinced even if someone rises from the dead." —*Lk 16:19-31*

Some critics object that this parable presumes to warn a public deaf to news of Jesus' rising, and so is wholly a Christian homiletic. Yet the Alexandrian Jewish original told no resurrection promise, but only how an unjust lifetime foolishly reaps disaster. Indeed, this storyteller echoes the Hebrew Bible ban on consulting the dead for future guidance, as Saul once fatally tried.[2] Instead, Abraham emphasizes here Jesus' consistent point that people already know all they need, and can respond to God's reign at once if only they will. Bar Maajan and his brothers are damned fools who should know better.

BRINGING YOUR CORNER

- *Do public reparations for injustice seem fair?*
- *What about convicts exonerated after police corrupted their trials long ago?*
- *If reparations are not possible, how can YOU act justly?*

D. THE JUBILEE AND LORD'S PRAYER

Premodern agriculture spread worldwide yet within tight natural margins. In lean years farmers must borrow for land taxes and seed, and to feed themselves, while bumper harvests came rarely. Moneylenders and taxmen prospered by exacting fat fees during hard times. Hence ratcheting spirals of debt merged small holdings inexorably into grand estates, which soon sparked power rivalries and dynastic change. No ancient treasury escaped debt's spiral for long, despite trying out new coinage, trade and plunder.

The Hebrew Bible's priestly writers command an innovative solution to growing wealth inequity, which some New Testament authors invoke in principle. That is the Jubilee, a fixed fiftieth year when all debts are wiped away and economies start over.[1]

Of course no society records obeying such a commandment —not because the rich oppose it, but because as that fiftieth year draws near, poor farmers cannot borrow for seed without soaring interest guarantees that no bumper crop could repay.

Hence the Jubilee ideal beckons from outside economic

reality. Proponents urge us to live by it nonetheless, and trust God to supply what we need, as prophets and psalmists tell us God has always done. Such Hebrew faith speaks up within other parables too. Jesus' voice is therefore one plausible strand among their chorus.

Saying #51 • *Flowers of the Field*
And why do you worry about clothing? Consider the lilies of the field, how they grow; they neither toil nor spin, yet I tell you, even Solomon in all his glory was not clothed like one of these. But if God so clothes the grass of the field, which is alive today and tomorrow is thrown into the oven, will he not much more clothe you—you of little faith? Therefore do not worry, saying, "What will we eat?" or "What will we drink?" or "What will we wear?" For it is the Gentiles who strive for all these things; and indeed your heavenly Father knows that you need all these things. But strive first for the kingdom of God and his righteousness, and all these things will be given to you as well. So do not worry about tomorrow, for tomorrow will bring worries of its own. Today's trouble is enough for today. —*Matt 6:28-29; Lk 12:27-28*

Saying #52 • *The Sun and the Rain*
Your Father in heaven makes his sun rise on the evil and on the good, and sends rain on the righteous and on the unrighteous... Be perfect, therefore, as your heavenly Father is perfect. —*Matt 5:45-48 (also James 1, Romans 3)*

Saying #53 • *Right and Left-Handed Alms*

> But when you give alms, do not let your left hand know
> what your right hand is doing... —*Matt 6:3*

God's incalculable blessing (*baruch/barakah*) falls in sunshine
and rain upon righteous and evil people's fields alike. Humans
flourish as the flowers do and are advised to benefit their
fellows the same way, not keeping score.

Almsgiving also works best without tabulation. Ancients
carried money in leather purses tied at the top. Since most
folks were right-handed, they held the purse in their left hand
and chose coins (by quick feel rather than sight) and
distributed them with the right. Their left hand reckons the
total by the weight of the purse, and so the gift that is
affordable.

This saying advises donors to give without pondering what
will remain. Many world teachers encourage generosity; yet
more, this teacher distinguishes what you need to know from
what you needn't know—a typical emphasis in Jesus' talk.

E. ALREADY FORGIVEN

Saying #54 • Lord's Prayer
Our Father in heaven, hallowed be your name. Your
kingdom come. Your will be done, on earth as it is in
heaven. Give us this day our bread *for tomorrow*. And
forgive us our debts, as we also have forgiven our
debtors. And do not bring us to the time of trial, but
rescue us from the evil one. —*Matt 6:9-13; Lk 11:2-4*

The "Lord's Prayer" is a composite by several first-
century Jewish teachers, who installed varying
parallel texts into synagogue worship. Yet both our
gospel versions do show emphases we tie to Jesus. Calling God
Our Father, or Aramaic *Abba* (Papa) is possibly Jesus' innovation: here critics differ.

More telling is his evocation of Moses' desert manna: give
us *today* the bread we need for *tomorrow*. In the Exodus story, a
day's manna might be collected in advance only on the
Sabbath eve, and if conserved afterward it would rot.[1] Such
urgent timing is typical of Jesus' voice, as we have noted

before. Jerome's Latin Vulgate rendered the synoptics' Greek in the style of John's gospel, without far-off future eschatology: "the Bread of Life." Today the Lord's Prayer and Jewish *Kaddish* (in all forms) reveal a many-colored prayer rug spread across biblical floors ancient and modern.

The need for forgiveness stressed in these prayers crosses zoological boundaries. Several species practice revenge as a means of defending their group.[2] Interviews find that many humans imagine they will feel better after taking revenge—but afterword most feel worse.[3] Hence outstanding Renaissance dramatists in England and Spain turn to forgiveness, in the face of a rampant fashion for revenge drama.[4]

Notably only one or two gospel verses counsel seeking forgiveness; most urge giving it. While some ancient versions of Luke's gospel lack the passage, others put these words into Jesus' mouth on the cross: "Forgive them, Father, they know not what they do." [5] Yet in fact most murderers do know what they do, just as Jesus warns we all already know what we need to know.

After the fall of South African racial apartheid, Christian President Nelson Mandela and Archbishop Desmond Tutu inaugurated Truth and Reconciliation Commissions in place of juridical tribunals. Wrongdoers could reenter free society if they admitted their crimes, so all would know. Such Commissions had been tried elsewhere and successfully avoided a bloodbath. On the other hand, surveys reveal that the public are only partly satisfied, while the eventual prosecution of Nazi criminals enjoys lasting public support.

Jesus' pattern of endurance and generosity is rare.[6] His flinty sayings never mention retaliation or restitution; one even advises not to ask for stolen things back.

BRINGING YOUR CORNER

- *What if a known culprit is never brought to trial?*
- *What about mob justice, America's 4000 lynchings?*
- *The same court verdict brings widely different sentences in Norway, USA and China. Whose justice is that?*

John Patton bases his provocative work *Is Human Forgiveness Possible?* on many years' experience guiding people through forgiveness processes. He argues the Church errs by pressing victims to forgive, and by so doing adds a tough obligation to their sense of injury. In practice, however, he finds forgiveness involves discovering that you *have* forgiven people and given up your desire to be separate from them. He understands human forgiveness *"not as doing something but as discovering something—that I am more like those who have hurt me than different from them. I am able to forgive when I discover that I am in no position to forgive."*[7] Just so, Matthew's text of the Lord's Prayer uses the perfect tense: forgive us as we *have forgiven* them."

Jesus' scandalous meals did not offer future reward for proper repentance; rather, they were welcoming Signs that God *has already forgiven* all humanity and holds no desire to be apart from us. Today when we watch people we think unworthy join our Eucharistic gathering, instead of telling ourselves we were misinformed and should reconsider how they deserve inclusion—we would do better to think: these are real, nasty, active sinners, and God sees no difference between them and me. I am just like them. So I hereby quit my desire to separate from them.

F. RENDERING WHAT TO WHOM?

Saying #55 • The Tax Coin
And they came and said to him, "Teacher, we know
that you are sincere, and show deference to no one; for
you do not regard people with partiality, but teach the
way of God in accordance with truth. Is it lawful to pay
taxes to Emperor *Caesar*, or not? Should we pay them,
or should we not?" But knowing their hypocrisy, he
said to them, "Why are you putting me to the test?
Bring me a denarius and let me see it." And they
brought one. Then he said to them, "Whose *image* is
this, and whose title?" They answered, "*Caesar's*." Jesus
said to them, "Give to *Caesar* the things that are
Caesar's, and to God the things that are God's." —*Mk
12:14-17; Matt 22:15-22; Lk 20:20-26*

Despite a canny solution by Gregory of Nyssa (long
overlooked), Jesus' tax coin simile confused
churches for centuries until Dorothy Sayers, a

modern theologian and mystery writer, unlocked it. Mystery novels often give clues in an opening chapter, which readers misunderstand. Then through hundreds of pages a sleuth pursues feints, false excuses and flimsy guesses until the solution appears as one that was open from the start.

Diverse interpreters have speculated for ages about what it is that Jesus is saying belongs to God and should be given to God. Our spiritual virtues perhaps? Our immortal souls? Our tithes? Our life commitments? Our moral conscience? Our conformance to church law? Through history, "give to Caesar" has confused preachers and canon lawyers who apologized for Caesar's needful claim on much of a Christian's life.

But mystery writer Sayers discovered that the dialog poses and solves a riddle. Jesus holds up the Roman coin, asking whose image it bears. Caesar's image is how we recognize its owner, they reply. Then what belongs to God must have the same proof. What bears God's image? You and I do: our whole human selves, as Genesis 2 declares. Then give your whole self to God, because you bear God's image.

Like our first parable group of ecstatic responses, or the parable of the pharisee and tax collector, this saying summons our immediate existential choice rather than eschatological postponement. It is a further flinty saying, reported in narrative form much the way that Hebrew authors retell the commandments credited to Moses. So Jesus is its likely first source, though another later storyteller may have elaborated the context we read here.

BRINGING YOUR CORNER

- *Have you ever ignored advice from a parent or lover, and then found the advice was right?*
- *Whom did you tell afterward?*
- *Did someone in this discussion clarify something that had puzzled you?*
- *Who has said something that struck you as new?*

G. FAITH IN GOSPEL STORIES

For the evangelists—and they imply for Jesus himself—an aggressive Faith in God's promises suffices for blessings, without Jewish doctrinal conformity or ethnic heritage or ritual affirmation. Gentiles and Jews alike are healed on account of their Faith;[1] schismatic Samaritans exemplify Faith;[2] disciples learn that their Faith in Christ is wholly a gift from God, and nothing they supply.[3] So the voiceless fig tree and flowers of the field set standards for human Faith.[4] For Paul, as we shall learn, Jesus' own Faith is the motive for his sacrificial death, and God rewards his faith with humankind's salvation.

BRINGING YOUR CORNER

- *Do you know people of another religion whose life shows their Faith?*

- *When people ask about your own Faith, what do you tell them?*
- *Is it comfortable to say?*

H. THE GREAT ASSIZE
TRIBUNAL

The Hebrew prophets' penalty for flouting God's reign is ruin. Amos, Isaiah, Jeremiah, and others warn that unless the nation changes plans and gives justice to the poor, it could be thrown onto a garbage heap like Gehenna, the smoldering pile steadily burning outside Jerusalem. Or cast out into freezing darkness, where shiverers moan and chatter their teeth.

These biblical punishments are grim but not eternal. David Bentley Hart finds eternal suffering absent from the Bible, which aims at redemption for all.[1] Hellish tortures cherished by medieval and baroque preachers arrived centuries after Jesus, borrowed from Hindus who prescribed painful cautery before one's next incarnation. Hindus are disgusted by this Christian adoption, however. They promise bliss once the purification/reincarnation process is completed—whereas Christianity has removed that promise, leaving eternal torment in its place.

Saying #56 • The Great Assize

When the Son of Man comes in his glory, and all the
angels with him, then he will sit on the throne of his
glory. All the nations will be gathered before him, and
he will separate people one from another as a shepherd
separates the sheep from the goats, and he will put the
sheep at his right hand and the goats at the left. Then
the king will say to those at his right hand, "Come, you
that are blessed by my Father, inherit the kingdom
prepared for you from the foundation of the world; for I
was hungry and you gave me food, I was thirsty and
you gave me something to drink, I was a stranger and
you welcomed me, I was naked and you gave me clothing, I was sick and you took care of me, I was in prison
and you visited me." Then the righteous will answer
him, "Lord, when was it that we saw you hungry and
gave you food, or thirsty and gave you something to
drink? And when was it that we saw you a stranger and
welcomed you, or naked and gave you clothing? And
when was it that we saw you sick or in prison and
visited you?" And the king will answer them, "Truly I
tell you, just as you did it to one of the least of these
who are members of my family, you did it to me." Then
he will say to those at his left hand, "You that are
accursed, depart from me into the eternal fire prepared
for the devil and his angels; for I was hungry and you
gave me no food, I was thirsty and you gave me nothing
to drink, I was a stranger and you did not welcome me,
naked and you did not give me clothing, sick and in
prison and you did not visit me." Then they also will
answer, "Lord, when was it that we saw you hungry or
thirsty or a stranger or naked or sick or in prison, and

did not take care of you?" Then he will answer them,
"Truly I tell you, just as you did not do it to one of the
least of these, you did not do it to me." And these will
go away into eternal punishment, but the righteous
into eternal life. —*Matt 25:31-46*

Self-blinded or feigned discovery of what the prophets
have long proclaimed is the plot engine driving Matthew's
most vivid doom parable: the Great Assize tribunal. Unlike
Jesus' own insistent emphasis upon decisions and results
today, the evangelist—like many Christian preachers—post-
pones this court process to Christ's return in final glory. Even
so, no story detail proves that the world we know has ended, or
human behavior changed.

Instead, this parable evokes a cyclical administrative event,
called in Greek *Parousia*, in Latin *Adventus* and in English
Assize, when a touring magistrate arrived regularly to suppress
crime, corruption and treason and firm up local loyalty to the
regime. Separating sheep from goats for feeding points to
normal ongoing village life. No animals are slaughtered here
for a final victory feast.

The parable's wealthy plunderers claim foolishly they did
not recognize God's image in poor humankind even though
their dispossession now is plain. For a hideous modern parallel, allied troops nearing Nazi Berlin in April 1945 met escapees
who urged them to liberate Buchenwald Concentration Camp
first. There soldiers discovered unimaginable suffering and
forced a thousand local townsfolk to march past twenty-one
thousand starving, skeletally emaciated Jews and political
prisoners. The townsfolk sobbed, "We didn't know! We had no
idea" of the camp's business. But the neighborhood signs had
been plain enough, and those nosy, gossipy villagers *did know*.

They were only forced to look now at what they and their fellow countrymen already well knew.

As the Nürnberg Nazi Museum shows, many leading Nazi war monsters escaped punishment thanks to US State Department anti-Semitism. And mass murderers in Cambodia, Rwanda, Serbia, Uganda and Myanmar have taken up their mantle in turn. Facing recurrent human depravity, a biblical definition of God's omnipotence offers one moral promise for us to rely upon: *I can work with anything.*

Despite the existential challenges we read among Jesus' sayings, and for all his affiliation with the poor, no image like Matthew's Great Assize tribunal appears elsewhere. Since this vivid threat might have fit well within Hebrew prophetic inheritance, the absence of an Assize echo elsewhere in Jesus' teaching is all the more remarkable. Perhaps given the low-lifes, opportunists and criminal malefactors among his listeners, and reflected in his parable heroes, the absence of legal arraignment stories is not surprising! One judge does appear, but only as a folk figure of official corruption.[2] (Saying 31: The Corrupt Judge.)

On the other hand, that absence points up a likely corner where Jesus risen awaits Paul for a meeting. As we shall see, Paul similarly replaces commonplace law court talk with living by Faith in God's friendship—something Adam failed to do, but Moses and Jesus did. And so must we. As St Isaac of Nineveh said in the 7th century: "Did not the Lord share the table of tax collectors and harlots? So then—do not distinguish between the worthy and unworthy. All must be equal in your eyes to love and to serve."

BRINGING YOUR CORNER

- *Which of Jesus' stories and sayings is your own personal favorite?*
- *Have you discovered anything new in this group conversation?*

I. LOVE'S SCANDAL

Some fellow explorers may wonder when we will hunt up Jesus' teaching about Love. Alas, we cannot follow those traces far. John's discourses on love color the synoptic ink sketches richly. For example, "No man can have greater love than to lay down his life for his friends" summarizes Jesus' chosen path until death.[1] But John's visionary mezzotint was written a full ancient lifetime after Jesus' crucifixion. More remarkably yet, while God's love fills the prophecies Jesus favored from Isaiah, Joel, Hosea, and Jeremiah, nonetheless the synoptic gospels offer no evidence Jesus preached about love as Paul would do. (See Saying #74 below.) They pursue a different theme crucial for both teachers.

We have seen how Jesus' sunniest sayings hint at opposing shadows, and many stories uphold mean protagonists. Gospel editors and preachers have dressed them up in handsome moral garb, though worshippers today may wonder what ethical truth they show. For instance, Jesus' story of the Entrusted Money,[2] translated into Tudor treasury terms, redefined the English word "talent" and soon advised each Christian to husband their gifts from God.[3] As if later tellers could revalue the rapacious crop thief's behavior! But Jesus and Paul have a bolder answer: love's scandal.

Anyone hearing warm encouragement from preachers today may marvel that Jesus' foes misheard him, while we no longer do. Yet crucifixion means more than rebuttal, and scandal means more than gossip. The Hebrew words translated as "scandal" or "stumbling block"[4] denote a snare or trap of offense. A part of the Levitical Holiness Code, which Judah Goldin says all synagogue schoolboys memorize, is normative for the New Testament: "You shall not curse the deaf, nor lay a stumbling block before the blind. I am YHWH."[5]

Nearly all references to a stumbling block in Hebrew and Greek scripture infer blindness. When prophet Jeremiah warns, "I will lay a stumbling block before this people," he is taunting them: My people are *blind!*[6] New Testament writers use the verb "lay a stumbling block" thirty times, twice as often as the noun, echoing the Levitical prohibition and so declaring: those who take offense are tragically blind and in danger.[7]

BRINGING YOUR CORNER

- *Have you ever done something you now think was foolish, whether lucky or not?*
- *Did you get away with it? Whose fault is that?*
- *Did someone else pay the price?*

Much like Isaiah and Jeremiah, Jesus chose his scandalous sign of common dining to seize his blundering people's attention before it was too late. And that scandal continues wherever Jesus shows up today. As the Lutheran writer Gordon Lathrop puts it: "Draw a line that includes us and excludes many others, and Jesus Christ is always on the other side of the line. At least that is so if we are speaking of the biblical, historic Christ who eats with sinners and outsiders, who is made a curse and sin itself for us, who justifies the ungodly, and who is himself the hole in any system."[8]

At every Christian liturgy, Jesus' Open Table feeds all the genuinely wrong guests together. This banquet serves for more than making people feel accepted, or building community, or growing churches. It serves for more than sharing gifts that baptized Christians can have, or faithful Trinitarians can have, or morally improved converts can have. Jesus' Open Table remains today a stumbling-block thrown down on our path, to teach a blind and reeling world what God is doing everywhere in this world, before it is too—damned—late.

Jesus' bald confrontational parables let us feel the offense his sign caused then—and its spiritual purpose. He knew the self-doomed took offense: "Blessed is anyone who does not stumble blindly over me."[9] His scandalous parables and his Welcoming Table sign alike were meant to stun people's eyes open.

Paul expressly extolls the scandal thrown down by Jesus' crucifixion. There he finds God's chief challenge to human vision. That tragic execution resembles Jeremiah's somber signs, meant to seize a whole nation's attention and change their plans. As we shall find in Part 7 below, Paul summoned yet more scripture to enlighten the views of unseeing rivals.

Passage #57 • God's Deliberate Scandal

For Jews demand signs, and Greeks desire wisdom, but
we proclaim Christ crucified, a *stumbling block* to Jews
and foolishness to gentiles, but to those who are called,
both Jews and Greeks, Christ the power of God and the
wisdom of God. For God's foolishness is wiser than
human wisdom, and God's weakness is stronger than
human strength. —*1 Cor 1:22-25*

PART FIVE
WOMEN FOR JESUS
AND PAUL

A. JESUS' BEST PUPILS THEN AND NOW

"Woman, great is your faith."
—*Matt 15:28*

In the gospel records of Jesus' teaching, women play a part different from contemporary authorities, and by implication even opposed. Jewish historians report that a rabbi must marry in order to obey the whole Law, so the evangelists' silence on this point implies that like Peter,[1] Jesus was duly married. Yet although the gospels prove his knowledge of children, they assign him none. Instead, Acts records the disciples' substitute choice of Jesus' brother to succeed him: an application of the Mosaic levirate. Thus Henry Chadwick observes that they spared his church all later contests over a caliphate, which perplex Islam violently to this day.[2]

On the other hand, the canonical gospels leave us no doubt that Jesus revered women. Proof shows in the one reliable charge we hear against him: the welcome attendance of harlots at his Welcoming Table sign.[3] Apart from ten little girls and one bungling housewife (Ten Bridesmaids and a Leaven

Maker, with their mixed successes) no females appear in Jesus' parables or flinty sayings. Several women do arise in narratives; but gospel stories come to us so highly edited that skeptical readers today mistrust their details. More tellingly, those tales show most men as blockheads, while women emerge as Jesus' top pupils. Canonical editors have kept this gender slant. It is plausible that the storytellers learned it from the teacher himself.

Although male characters in some authentic parables may be copied after notorious actual felons (the Dishonest Rent-Collector, the Crop Thief's Entrusted Money, the Man with Two Sons) our evangelists' tales of women are more circumspect, and we can assume their actors are fictional. Indeed, several of their plots echo Jesus' parables in a different way. Hence Confucius' method of shared exploration will serve us here as well. Finding and bringing our own matching corners demands actual life experiences, rather than fictive imagination. Therefore let me offer real parallel examples from our own era to stimulate group members' memories. Most retold here are Anglicans, but not all.

Story and Saying #58 • *Genital Bleeding Healed*

Now there was a woman who had been suffering from hemorrhages for twelve years. She had endured much under many physicians and had spent all that she had; and she was no better, but rather grew worse. She had heard about Jesus and came up behind him in the crowd and touched his cloak, for she said, "If I but touch his clothes, I will be made well." Immediately her hemorrhage stopped; and she felt in her body that she was healed of her disease. Immediately aware that power had gone forth from him, Jesus turned about in the crowd and said, "Who touched my clothes?" And

his disciples said to him, "You see the crowd pressing in
on you; how can you say, 'Who touched me?'" He
looked all round to see who had done it. But the
woman, knowing what had happened to her, came in
fear and trembling, fell down before him, and told him
the whole truth. He said to her, "Daughter, your Faith
has made you well; go in peace, and be healed of your
disease." —*Mark 5:25-34*

This narrative exemplifies first century debates over ritual
pollution. Breaking the common taboo, a woman with a flow
of genital blood touches Jesus' robe—an action he discovers
only by sensing that healing power has left his body.[4] Looking
at a number of Jesus' healings, Thiessen observes that such
effects upon a lethal source of human uncleanness always
demonstrate Jesus' opposition to the forces of death.[5]

On the other hand, this woman is the grammatical actor
for eighteen verbs (whether active or passive) whereas Jesus'
one declared deed is welcoming the aggression that proves her
Faith. We may recall Jesus' short saying about violent people
getting into God's reign,[6] along with at least three parable
actors who trample hallowed custom. The friend begging food
at midnight and the corrupt judge know what settled rules are
broken, but circumstances afford little choice.[7] The man with
two sons outwits his scandalized neighbors to preserve his
family, even at his older son's cost.[8]

Like those men, the bleeding woman knows what her life
needs, and she proves quick and ready the way Jesus' table
companions and parable heroes do, while more upright
resisters hang back. Her instant aggression brings success—an
outstanding parable emphasis.

BRINGING YOUR CORNER

- *Are some truths you know more important to you than others?*
- *Has overlooking injustice or insult ever worked in your favor?*
- *Have you learned good ways to avoid saying "I told you so"?*

FIRST MODERN PARALLEL: TWO QUICK AND READY ENGLISH CHURCHWOMEN

Valiant British physician **Cecily Saunders** overturned the standard treatment of dying people. Instead of stressing physical survival as the overriding goal of medicine, whatever its cost in prolonged suffering, she founded London's St. Christopher's Hospice in 1967 to serve dying people's personal needs foremost. Readily prescribing painkiller drugs, and welcoming family attendance—measures ruled out at established hospitals—Dr. Saunders overcame entrenched professional resistance and sparked the worldwide hospice movement. Her work now benefits sufferers in countless countries as they approach our common human finality. Among many honors, Queen Elizabeth II created her Dame Cecily Saunders of the British Empire in 1979. She died of cancer at her own St. Christopher's Hospice in 2005.

As the mystifying HIV virus and AIDS spread uncontrolled among the North American gay male population, arousing public fear and ostracism, Franciscan **Sister Ruth Hall** opened San Francisco's Family Link in a vacant commercial tower: there she offered free hospitality to relatives who came long distances to attend their dying sons. Sister Ruth's blunt County Durham frankness earned the support of city officers and donors alike, and by the time she died in 2020, she and her volunteers had hosted nearly a thousand grieving family members.

Wondrous healings like the Bible tells were beyond these women's power, yet they transformed society's treatment of despised people helplessly sick.

BRINGING YOUR CORNER

- *Do you know women like Dame Cecily and Sister Ruth?*
- *Have you worked on a suicide hotline or affordable counseling service?*
- *Do you know someone who has?*

Story and Saying #59 • Martha and Mary
Now as they went on their way, he entered a certain village, where a woman named Martha welcomed him into her home. She had a sister named Mary, who sat at the Lord's feet and listened to what he was saying. But Martha was distracted by her many tasks; so she came to Jesus and asked, "Lord, do you not care that my sister has left me to do all the work by myself? Tell her then to help me." But the Lord answered her, "Martha, Martha, you are worried and distracted by many things; there is need of only one thing. Mary has chosen the best *piece*, which will not be taken away from her."
—Lk 10:38-42

Luke's story of two sisters Martha and Mary—the one laboring, the other listening[9]—has been misread for centuries to say God favors a contemplative lifestyle above an active one. On the contrary, here is another aggression story, with a provocative extra twist: plain injustice cannot disqualify one's eager response to God.

As above, readers must notice the *verbs* first. Jesus admits Martha *works* well, rightly deserving assistance. But Mary has *chosen* the best slice of their cake[10] (perhaps the slice with the extra frosting rose), and even if unfairly *seized*, that treasure shall in no case be *taken* from her—or by implication, *taken* from anyone else.

Mary in this story is like the child in Jesus' shortest parable, *seizing* what she *prizes* no matter who might object,[11] or like the parable employer who *answers* disgruntled day-laborers that he *has* a right to *spend* his own money however he *likes*.[12] The man with two sons likewise reckons: if I can *save* my younger son from village outrage and revenge, justice and custom be *damned*. That parable's unjust father *withstands* death's threatening power just as Jesus' healing does. In the same way, Mary's very injustice to Martha underscores her *grasping* the truth that Jesus hopes all will *catch*.

Women in two further gospel narratives exemplify Jesus' distinctive views.

SECOND MODERN PARALLEL: A CAMPAIGNING AMERICAN CHURCHWOMAN

Unlike all the women in Jesus' parables, Episcopalian **Eleanor Roosevelt** was born to wealth and privilege. When her husband (and cousin) Franklin was elected President of the

United States, she encouraged his liberal ideals, and worked to advance political change on her own initiative. She opposed interning Japanese American citizens during World War II and championed Native American rights. Her relentless witness for helpless people "chose the good part" on their behalf, and led to permanent legal changes.

BRINGING YOUR CORNER

- *Have you known women like Eleanor Roosevelt?*
- *Are progressive politicians sincere? How can you tell?*

Story and Saying #60 • An Adulteress Forgiven
The scribes and the Pharisees brought a woman who had been caught in adultery; and making her stand before all of them, they said to him, "Teacher, this woman was caught in the very act of committing adultery. Now in the law Moses commanded us to stone such women. Now what do you say?" They said this to test him, so that they might have some charge to bring against him. Jesus bent down and wrote with his finger on the ground. When they kept on questioning him, he straightened up and said to them, "Let anyone among you who is without sin be the first to throw a stone at her." And once again he bent down and wrote on the ground. When they heard it, they went away, one by one, beginning with the elders; and Jesus was left alone with the woman standing before him. Jesus straightened up and said to her, "Woman, where are they? Has

no one condemned you?" She said, "No one, sir." And Jesus said, "Neither do I condemn you. Go your way, and from now on do not sin again." —*Jn 8:3-11*

This woman taken for adultery hears verbal forgiveness, which Jesus' prophetic table sign showed openly toward sinners in general. His rhetorical question in the grammatical passive voice implies that forgiveness is divine: "Has no one condemned you? Then neither do I."[13]

BRINGING YOUR CORNER

- *Is it possible to work with people without judgment?*
- *Do you favor closing prisons? Profit-making prisons?*
- *How shall we address the feelings of crime victims?*

Story and Saying #61 • It is Too Fair!
A woman whose little daughter had an unclean spirit immediately heard about him, and she came and bowed down at his feet. Now the woman was a Gentile, of Syrophoenician origin. She begged him to cast the demon out of her daughter. He said to her, "Let the children be fed first, for it is not fair to take the children's food and throw it to the dogs." But she answered him, "*Oh yes it is too fair! Because* even the dogs under the table eat the children's crumbs." Then he said to her, "For saying that, you may go—the demon has left your daughter." So she went home, found the child lying on the bed, and the demon gone. —*Mk 7:25-30*

In this equally dramatic story, familiar mistranslation can obscure the evangelist's Hebrew scriptural echo. A Philistine woman (Israel's historic rival populace) rebuts Jesus' refusal to heal her gentile daughter as unfair, so Jesus relents, and heals the girl. Pious interpreters have misread the mother's reply as a polite plea for an exception, but instead, the Greek text grammar shows she contradicts Jesus bluntly and absolutely. *"Oh yes it is too fair! Because* even the dogs below eat scraps falling from the children's table."[14]

This is a classic Jewish *halakah,* wherein a teacher appears to discover his most famous doctrine through correction. Mark's storyteller summons up an aggressive pagan woman to teach us what the evangelist knows Jesus taught above all: no one is outside God's reign. (Likewise Paul will insist along with the Bible's prophets, that God plays no national favorites.)[15]

THIRD MODERN PARALLEL: A TENACIOUS SOUTH AFRICAN DEBATER

Like all the women in Jesus' parables, South African **Helen Sussman** was a Jew. Elected and re-elected to Parliament, she spoke out tirelessly against her government's racist Apartheid policies and befriended black Anglican Archbishop Desmond Tutu. Dutch Calvinist President Piet Botha complained that her speeches embarrassed the country, and she replied, "It is you who embarrass South Africa!" After Apartheid fell in 1991, Botha apologized, telling her she had been right about the truth, and right to reprove injustice to all people as openly as the Philistine woman had done in Jesus' hearing.

BRINGING YOUR CORNER

- *Have you lost an argument to a parent or spouse or friend of the opposite gender?*
- *Do you habitually assume an arguer of your own gender is right—at least at first?*
- *Were you persuaded to change your mind?*
- *Would you assume the reverse next time?*

Story and Saying #62 • Fleeing Disciples
All of them deserted him and fled. —*Mk 14:50; Matt 26:56*

Story and Saying #63 • The Empty Tomb
When the sabbath was over, Mary Magdalene, and Mary the mother of James, and Salome bought spices, so that they might go and anoint him. And very early on the first day of the week, when the sun had risen, they went to the tomb. They had been saying to one another, 'Who will roll away the stone for us from the entrance to the tomb?' When they looked up, they saw that the stone, which was very large, had already been rolled back. As they entered the tomb, they saw a young man, dressed in a white robe, sitting on the right side; and they were alarmed. But he said to them, 'Do not be alarmed; you are looking for Jesus of Nazareth, who was crucified. He has been raised; he is not here. Look, there is the place they laid him. But go, tell his disciples and Peter that he is going ahead of you to Galilee; there you will see him, just as he told you.' So they went out and fled from the tomb, for terror and amazement had

seized them; and they said nothing to anyone, for they were afraid. —*Mk 6:1-8*

The gospel passions contain our earliest narrative matter, though with early sermon comment already added in. Mark's gospel reports that at Jesus' arrest, all his disciples forsook him. Symbolic tales about those disciples' acts thereafter are not provable history; nonetheless four evangelists concur that women knew Jesus' resurrection first, however that conviction came to them, and these later instructed the doubting males. [16]

Although the synoptic gospels introduce an encouraging angelic messenger, no secret hidden knowledge is uncovered there. Writing a generation before the gospel evangelists, Paul reminded Roman Jews: this is the sort of God who raises the dead and brings out things that do not exist yet.[17] Much the way Jesus had preached during his lifetime, the gospels' female witnesses to his resurrection teach Bible theology everyone should already know.

FOURTH MODERN PARALLEL: A REVOLUTIONARY AMERICAN CHURCHWOMAN

Many American school children learn of blind and deaf **Helen Keller**'s rescue from speechless isolation through the guidance of ingenious teacher Anne Sullivan. Keller authored fourteen books and hundreds of speeches and essays, and won recognition worldwide. A devout Episcopalian, she campaigned for people with disabilities, for women's suffrage, labor rights, and world peace. She joined the Socialist Party of America in 1909, was a supporter of the National Association for the Advancement of Colored People (NAACP) and an original member of the American Civil Liberties Union. Like the women who went to bury Jesus, she brought life-saving news for her country out of her own tragedy and loss.

BRINGING YOUR CORNER

- *Do you know women like Helen Sussman and Helen Keller*
- *What would they ask you to do now? How would you respond?*

B. PAUL'S CHRISTIAN WOMEN FRIENDS

Saying #64 • Neither Male nor Female in Christ
As many of you as were baptized into Christ have
clothed yourselves with Christ. There is no longer Jew
or Greek, there is no longer slave or free, there is no
longer male and female; for all of you are one in Christ
Jesus. —*Gal 3:27-28*

We have read how a rabbi must marry in order to
keep the whole law. Some advocated conjugal sex
daily, and twice on the Sabbath. Although Paul's
letters defend his bachelor missionary style, he was married
for certain during some part of his life.[1] In 1 Corinthians 9 he
refers to his wife (whom some translations call his "companion") and complains that he and Barnabas should be compen-
sated for their expenses just as Peter and the Twelve are, so
they too can afford to bring their wives with them. Several
early writers also affirm Paul's married state. Paul never claims
children, however, and perhaps was widowed later.

Women's eminence within the rich fabric of Jesus' company outshines Paul's social anxieties about their speaking up and marrying.[2] Those predictably dismay modern readers; yet even so, Paul declares friendship and admiration for women in his gentile churches, naming them gratefully like men.[3] Perhaps to balance his patriarchal social standard and pugilistic male arguing style, half his letters end by singling out women for praise and thanks, three repeatedly. Afterward, our gospels and epistles attest to women's lasting leadership in the very same early Christian congregations that Paul knew —leadership which spread as rich Roman matrons hosted churches, which then built basilicas bearing their names forever.

FIFTH MODERN PARALLEL: A PIONEERING CHINESE CHURCHWOMAN

Just before the Japanese navy invaded Hong Kong in 1941, Anglican **Li Tim Oi** was ordained a woman deacon, empowered to guarantee sacramental worship for Chinese Christians if British colonial clergy were exiled or shot. The Japanese forbade a woman's public ministry, and the postwar Chinese Communist and British governments continued the Japanese ban. Imprisoned during China's Cultural Revolution, Li saw her priesthood formally confirmed at Hong Kong in 1971. Thereafter she emigrated to Toronto and undertook service in the Anglican Church of Canada until her death in 1992. Over her resolutely faithful lifetime of 84 years, Li witnessed the complete return of women to all the orders of church ministry that both genders had anciently exercised together.

Florence Li Tim Oi, the first Anglican woman ordained Priest.
Fresco by Mark Dukes

BRINGING YOUR CORNER

- *Have you known women like Li Tim Oi?*
- *Have you other women heroes? In your own family?*
- *Did they see their patient labors fulfilled?*

PART SIX
JESUS' AUTHORITY

Saying #65
"For this I came." —*Jn 18:37*

During a Chicago rally against the North American Vietnam War, a young Buddhist demonstrator challenged New York Senator Robert Kennedy, "What would you do if *your* son was drafted?" Over the loudspeaker, the former US Attorney General and current presidential candidate answered: "Next Question!"[1] Until martyred early in his electoral cause, Kennedy had voters pondering one stark query: Who is this man, and what authority should we give him?

All religious parties face that question about Jesus. Despite modern evangelical pretensions to teach one coherent biblical moral standard, the bible actually records important disputes among authorities. When Hebrew literary prophecy first appeared, most prophets were shrine personnel, like pagan soothsayers. Prophet Amos starts his work at Israel's Bethel sanctuary with a blistering broadside against international bloodletting that would have done any Levitical moralist proud.[2] But the priest Amaziah shoos Amos away from his royally established shrine, lest God take offence at any stain on King Jeroboam II's sacred charge. He orders Amos to prophesy doom somewhere else. Their authority conflict spells awful ruin for Amaziah and his whole family.[3]

On the other hand, some traditionalist divines dismiss historians by saying: Jesus is gone; the Church has the universal Christ now and can speak for him—just ask the Church's councils! Yet that would mean jettisoning the New Testament altogether, since those documents were written to tell us *who it is that is here.*

A. GROUP LIFE: TAVISTOCK

After World War II, Tommy Wilson, Edwin Bion and other researchers at London's Tavistock Institute revised common concepts of group behavior. Based on years of clinical research, they defined Authority simply: *The ability to do work.*

BRINGING YOUR CORNER

- *Have you received degrees authorizing you for work?*
- *Are you doing that work now, or very different work?*

Following Freud's skeptical principle that human response rarely means what it seems, Tavistock scholars distinguish Authority from Power, which can be resisted openly. Authority requires a social compact, so resistance is informal and typically covert.

When Corsican general Napoleon Bonaparte liberated Italy (as he thought) for the French Enlightenment, he told a local aristocrat, *"Principessa, noi Francesi non siamo tutti diavoli."* (We Frenchmen are not all devils.) Wittily she countered him with his own name, *"No, ma buona parte!"* Today democratic voters wonder at the loyalty of monarchy subjects', whose hereditary royals are feckless, inept, lazy, cruel, and stupid—and yet who enjoy the devotion of thousands eager to fight and die for their honor.

"Don't you see," Napoleon used to say to members of his family, "that I was not born to the throne, that I have to maintain myself on it in the same way I ascended to it, with [battle] glory, that it has to keep growing, that an individual who becomes a sovereign, like me, cannot stop, that he has to keep climbing, and that he is lost if he remains still."[1]

Sigmund Freud located the cause deep in our human consciousness:

"I have said that we [psychoanalysts] have much to expect from the increase in Authority which must accrue to us as time goes on. I need not say much to you about the importance of Authority. Only very few civilized people are capable of existing without reliance on others or are even capable of coming to an independent opinion. You cannot exaggerate the intensity of people's inner lack of resolution and craving for Authority. *The extraordinary increase in neuroses since the power of religions has waned may give you a measure of it.* The impoverishment of the ego due to the large expenditure of energy on repression, demanded of every individual by civilization, may be one of the principal causes of this state of things."[2]

BRINGING YOUR CORNER

- *Have ancestors in your family history taken actions you wouldn't take today?*
- *Do you like some customs you inherit? Dislike some?*

———————

Far more than the streams of blood sacrifice, substitutionary atonement and apocalyptic myth that would later drown Western Church discourse, authority floods the New Testament. All four canonical gospels describe Jesus debating this lone issue. As the synoptics quote him: "If you will not tell me by whose authority John baptized, neither will I tell you on whose authority I do these things."[3]

Thiessen shows Jesus upholds both Levitical and prophetic tradition, along with many rabbis.[4] Biblical prophets did not condemn ritual, but rather the marriage of pious ceremonies with injustice.[5] The priestly authors of Leviticus—their contemporaries—wholly concurred, and ancient readers would not have distinguished two sets of ritual versus social commandments, but one.[6]

In Jesus' Good Samaritan parable, the pilgrim priest and Levite first show tentative interest, "eyeing" the fallen robbery victim—and then make the wrong ethical choice to preserve ritual purity alone, as few ancient rabbis would advise them to do. Thus they yield cultic authority as well as power to the robbers—and so to the forces of death, Jesus' top target as a healer. John's gospel skirts ritual questions, instead offering long discourses that proclaim Jesus' authority to speak for God.[7] Like Jesus, Samaritans never opposed sacred ritual, but only the human clerical authority that presumed to govern and enforce it. Critic Raymond Brown identifies John's gospel with a Samaritan Christian community[8] and Thiessen observes that John's gospel alone omits ritual purity debate.[9] Creating a Samaritan hero, Jesus' sedition stands proud, and his contest over scripture resounds even today. When healing a paralytic, the Synoptics' Jesus asserts radically but simply:

Saying #66 • *Human Authority*
"*A human like myself* has authority on earth to forgive sins." —Mk 2:11[10]

That crucial issue weaves through the New Testament's kaleidoscopic tapestry. **Critical readers** may draw out dark threads of violence, blood sacrifice, ethnic singularity, patriarchy, and noble truths found in other faiths. Nonetheless, this Christian fabric is dyed deep with God's authority throughout.

B. KNOWING AN ORIGINAL MAN WHEN YOU SEE ONE

Saying #67 • *Born to Testify to the Truth*
Pilate: "So you are a king, then."
Jesus: "*Who told you that?* ...You say that I am a king. For this I was born, and for this I came into the world, to testify to the truth."[1]
"Truth?" said Pilate, "What is that?" —*Jn 18:37*

We have studied sixty-five sayings attributed to Jesus: all critically tried, arguably authentic, and arranged from joyful to confrontational. Now we can engage one question that opened this book. How might Jesus' teaching have led to his death? Our arrangement was our own artifice, erected to spy his thoughts, darkening as his final contest approached. The gospel editors may have hazarded something similar, and modern readers hunt for a sociopolitical agenda underneath. Yet both bright and dark colors reemerge throughout these tales, obscuring a steady drift. Instead, we can now offer a surprise conclusion to our search: Pilate the Governor alone got Jesus and his foes right.[2]

Mark reports that Pilate knew Jesus' accusers had delivered him from envy *(dia phthonon)*.[3]

Envy—rather than Pride, the medieval favorite—is the Bible's Original Sin. It overreaches jealousy, which says simply "I want something you have." Envy says, "I want you not to have it, whether or not I might win it in your stead." The machinery of envy does not require difference in wealth, power, or social prestige. Many envious attacks come from equals. My envious heart believes that available rewards and honors cannot guarantee me a proper share; so I attack any potential rival, whether or not my own share will grow thereby. Our world of scarcity can arouse ubiquitous human jealousies, where the fittest all scramble to survive. Those grounds of jealousy can grow, matching life's shifting novelties. But Envy is less logical, and requires a plain competitive longing. The chief priests had such bare grounds to envy Jesus, which the mob picked up and enlarged from their own envious hearts. Perhaps only the Resurrection's abundance can flood away the grounds for our human envy machine.

Adrian Van Kamm names Originality as Envy's top target,[4] because original actions and honors are newly minted, so that we cannot train beforehand to compete. In a world of fresh creativity, Jesus found—as Abel found in Cain's great Original Crime—that the weapons of envy are the weapons of death.

BRINGING YOUR CORNER

- *Have you seen envy at work up close? Or on a national public scale?*
- *Have you struggled against envy within yourself?*

- *Has novelty or brilliance made you reflexively suspicious?*

Originality soaks Jesus' teaching fabric. His constant Table Fellowship, where the clean and unclean dined united, was an original appropriation of Isaiah's prophecy that no one copied. And his provocative stories also gave Originality persistent prominence.

Singularly inventive actors abound there. The Pearl Merchant knew the rarest pearl's value as its owners did not *(Saying #12, above)*. The divinely lucky Moneychanger won a surprise fortune from his customer's ignorance *(#13)*. The Gardener knew to give an apparently barren tree one more chance (#14). The ploughman wrongly hid a found Treasure from the public eye so he could buy the field *(#20)*. The Wheat Farmer resisted his workers' obvious advice and so saved his crop *(#16)*. The Generous Employer acted willfully apart from popular fairness *(#18)*. The Cheating Rent-Collector ruined his boss while securing the sharecroppers and his own future *(#27)*. Half the Bridesmaids and the Groom joined forces to save the wedding night *(#29)*. The justified Tax Collector skipped a penitent's expected pledge to reform *(#35)*. A lone Samaritan traveler outshone the clergy pilgrims *(#47)*. Even the Foolish Housewife *(#25)* and the miserly Rich Farmer *(#28)* created distinctive blunders that Jesus' stories render proverbial.

Jesus was an Original Man who told tales about original folk. Some were generous, some wicked; some were bold, some devious; some were astute, some reckless—but in their contexts each was highly original. Over Jesus' two short preaching years, so much originality drew an inevitable envious response.

The four canonical Passion stories supply our earliest narrative material about him. Historians sidestep fulfilled prophecies there, and listen for singular details. Intuiting that Jesus was harmless, Pilate offered him a commonplace court-room quarrel as a way out; but *praüs* Jesus stonily declined it. (No wonder Muslims title Jesus *Ul al-Asm*, "one of the steadfast ones.") All along he knew his danger, though critics doubt Jesus could have foreseen his crucifixion sentence. Yet his *praüs* flinty faithfulness was no flaw, nor was his death a classic tragedy. His famed storytelling rhetoric and powerful kindness when healing sufferers only made him envy's target all the more. Pilate pronounced in the end—not a moralist's judgment on Jesus, but a historian's judgment:

Saying #68 • Pilate's Truth
"You take him yourselves and crucify him, for I find no fault in him." —*Jn 19:6*

PART SEVEN
PAUL'S AUTHORITY

Saying #69 • *God's Truth*
"Though everyone is a liar, let God be proved true."
—*Rom 3:4*

Jesus' parables invoke such existential choices as every human must make, whereas Paul's letters to gentile churches fix foremost on their community life. His letter to the Romans addresses Jews as a body, and so opens with a quick bid for that group's authority. Commentaries can brush over those first six verses too quickly. Authority is our issue, as it was Paul's opening issue.

Paul's opening six verses of Romans declare that Jesus is God's authoritative *Messiah* (Hebrew for Anointed, or "Christ" in Greek) that Jews have been looking for. If they have awaited a royal successor to national military champion David, says Paul, Jesus had David's genes. (Respect for heritage remains a factor in choosing leaders today.) If they search for a fresh spiritual movement, God signed the papers authorizing Jesus by raising him from the dead and spreading his spirit to do work everywhere. Jesus' resurrection proves his authority henceforward, and confers it upon his followers as well, whether they witnessed his short lifetime ministry or not. (Paul had not, nor have we.)

Even the surprise of a crucified Messiah has biblical precedent. Romans 1:3 cites heritage from David as Jesus' first messianic credential. Yet young David's personal authority had utterly surprised his family, his ordaining prophet Samuel, the giant Goliath, and King Saul, whose children supported David instead of their father. All those were blind to David's native gifts and divine appointment. In the same way Paul says (1 Cor. 1:23) the Jews at first were blind to a suffering Messiah. (Paul's "stumbling block" means blindness, as explained above.)

Indeed, blindness to scripture remains today's problem. Said Roman Catholic liturgist Ralph Kiefer: "The Word of God is not the Bible. The Word of God is what God says to the Church when the Bible is read." Barely fifteen decades ago, defenders of chattel slavery quoted the Bible lavishly, while abolitionists from Gregory of Nyssa to Sojourner Truth appealed to scripture too. Today some evangelicals quote Bible verses against social change, while progressives deny their authority to interpret the Bible so.

Fordham University's George MacCauley SJ, a leading Tavistock researcher and trainer, blazed a group psychology trail into the forest of Paul's letters about Christian common life, particularly his Roman letter. Drawing upon Tavistock studies that detect disguise and self-deception cloaking human behavior, MacCauley taught students to read scripture on bald contemporary terms.[1] Here again, let us apply Confucius' method. Answer the questions below without invoking theory; instead unearth your own corners of life experience, and bring them to fold with others'.

BRINGING YOUR CORNER

- *Do you vote as your parents did?*
- *Do you cherish long-term friends with whom you no longer agree?*
- *Does the School Board say what your children should read?*

A. WHO IS PAUL?

I f Saul of Tarsus, also called Paul, knew anything of Jesus' teaching, his letters do not say so. If Jesus worked wonders healing and casting out demons, Paul did not witness those. Did Paul sift and weigh the historical Jesus like a modern investigator? He argues otherwise. Nevertheless, Paul's examples are all historically concrete: Abraham, Moses, Jesus, Paul himself.

Even when he names Hellenistic abstractions about universal powers, those powers do not represent God's grand purpose (Greek *logos*). Along with other New Testament speakers, Paul proclaims Jesus' sole authority in action. We have seen how Tavistock group psychology defines authority throughout all human cultures as: the ability to do work. Then what work does Paul do? Indeed, who is Paul?

We know more about Paul than Jesus. It would be two centuries before Jewish rabbis consolidated their training at Persian Babylon, but some historians infer that Jesus' arguments aligned with their young emerging movement: a devout minority reviving Jewish culture along the lines of Hebrew scripture.[1] Paul was a Palestinian pharisee, a sometime pupil of famous Sanhedrin authority Gamaliel, and at first he persecuted Jesus' surviving fellowship.

At some point he switched sides, however, and began preaching that their executed rabbi was the nation's long-awaited messiah (king), now newly alive and powerful thanks to his Faith. That strategy change amazed Jesus' followers and earned Paul the same Jewish resistance he himself had formerly raised. More surprising yet, he began preaching to ethnically distinct (hence ritually impure) gentiles: people whom few among Paul's rabbinical fellows proselytized, and none of Jesus' table fellowships enrolled.[2]

BRINGING YOUR CORNER

- *Did you try other paths before the one you are on now?*
- *What do you treasure from any of them, that you have brought here with you?*

B. FOR WHOM DOES PAUL WRITE?

R hetoric means persuasion, and good persuaders know their hearers. To fathom Paul's thesis, we must divine who he presumed was listening. Unlike Jesus, Paul left us ten full letters arguing immediate issues, often in high dudgeon too. Each addresses a specific community, as at Corinth, Philippi, or Galatia, although their arguments merge, since he founded the lot.

The Roman congregation was founded by others, however. Scholars today argue whether this final letter to the Roman church addresses a Jewish readership, a convert gentile body, or a mixed congregation. All are possible, since the Jewish diaspora in Rome surpassed Jerusalem in population—much as Irish in Massachusetts now outnumber those near Dublin. Nonetheless, Paul's rhetoric fits one audience most snugly.

Some critics favor gentile recipients, proposing that Paul invoked his authority as "ordained" apostle to the gentiles.[1] But resistance and contest actually fill Paul's gentile church letters.[2] Decades later in Acts, we read of Paul locked in authority wrangles within congregations he founded. Why would Roman gentiles who had never met him yield to such a conflicted authority claim?

Moreover, when writing to gentile readers elsewhere, Paul handily invokes the competitive sports that quickened Greco-Roman civic life: boxing, training, and running.[3] He is a fighter, with a taste for combat, possibly a joy in it. Commentators rarely notice Paul's references to athletic contest (boxing, racing, etc.) where competitive combat is popular. Most medieval and modern academics prefer the library. Paul alludes to sports more than to philosophical discussion, where text commentators feel more at home. Athletic and prize-winning metaphors do recur in the post-Pauline letters to the Hebrews and Ephesians[4]—as well as Christian exhortations during persecutions, and apologies for monasticism afterward. But Paul's Roman letter singularly mentions none.

Paul knew that Jewish readers would hardly welcome them anyhow. Despite the Hebrew Bible's wrestling patriarchs,[5] rabbis commonly opposed the games,[6] and their Roman pupils presumably learned their view. Indeed, Paul's harsh caricature of pagan games and theatre audiences at Romans 1:32 shows what prejudice he expects to meet, and (disingenuously?) he echoes it. He declares his missionary authority tactfully, and without competitive tone. Indeed, Paul turns from condemning gentile religion (as some ancient prophets did) to come alongside his readers:

Saying #70 • *Paul Reproves Jewish Resistance*
"Do you despise the riches of God's forbearance and patience? Do you not realize that God's kindness is meant to lead you to repentance?" —*Rom 2:4*

That is the theology of Hebrew prophet Joel, crucial to

Jesus' central Pharisee and Tax Collector parable—a theology distinctive in Judaism, and affirmed by Jesus and Paul equally.

BRINGING YOUR CORNER

- *Have you joined in a late-night religious argument, perhaps during college?*
- *Did anyone change their mind? Why?*
- *Are you still friends with an opponent?*

This rhetoric plainly marks out his fellow Jewish readers as Paul's target. Without propounding Joel's doctrine he briefly paraphrases it—the earliest form of quotation—even though it fills a central role in his ensuing soliloquy, which he presumes readers will follow and understand.

No gentile reader could have grasped him so easily, because gentile religion taught nothing similar. Ramsay MacMullen shows that apart from popular dancing and singing (the early Church's strongest continuity with paganism),[7] popular religion cooked a gristly stew of soothsaying, talismans, curses, and threatened payback by some ravenous god for any careless omissions. Vengeful underground Furies never forgave; and even the heroic favorites of gods from atop Mt Olympus died their dark doom whenever the weaving Fates decreed it. Thiessen rebuts Christian critics who accuse rabbis of ethnocentric or legalistic demands. Those critics might better declare how such a constricted Judaism as they describe could have lured gentile converts, whose own tradition bequeathed them a faith already grim enough.

For example, to render the Hebrew concept *tsedaqah* (YHWH God putting right what is wrong), the Greek Septuagint translators ventured *dikaiosynê*, the work of Homeric goddess Dikê mending the boundary between gods and mortals when broken by human presumption or godly sexual congress. A deadly theological pitfall lurks there, however: unlike Hebrew YHWH, Olympic Dikê never forgives. Her ministrations always disempower the gods and ruin the mortal wretches involved.

By bright contrast, Jewish worship provides ready means to obtain YHWH's forgiveness, and editors long before Paul had stamped Joel's theology of YHWH patiently awaiting our repentance a dozen times around Hebrew Scripture.[8] Those editors envisioned a benign deity even when warning errant Israel. Forgiveness became the principal mechanism of regular temple worship, and the promised fruit of prophecy long after Joel.

In Paul's Roman letter, Hebrew prophecy resounds. His opening chapters formally echo the prophet Amos, who stunningly recites how pagans earn punishment, and then (for seven more chapters) warns how Jews surprisingly court the same doom.[9] Amos' resonant rhetoric summoned Jewish ears to hear his thunderous counterpoint, and Paul presumes his Roman listeners will recall the full tragic chorale. Thiessen catches a similar lament echoed from Jeremiah.[10] Much as Mozart's *Don Giovanni* quoted Vienna's hottest popular opera tune, something written by his librettist Da Ponte,[11] Paul expects his Roman readers to recognize prophetic melodies as soon as they hear them. By comparison, the prophets sound sparingly in his gentile church letters. Like a skilled music teacher, Paul knows which scores different pupils can readily read.

BRINGING YOUR CORNER

- *Have you attended a bar mitzvah or bat mitzvah?*
- *Do you know anyone who married someone with a different faith tradition?*
- *Have they told you about any of their talk around shared values?*

C. HIS TRUE
TRANSFORMATION

Luke's paired biographies of Jesus and Paul blend in classical Christian oratory from the next century, when Luke wrote. Wonder tales and common sermons were standard hagiography for him. Luke's dramatic account of Paul's change of heart when nearing Damascus, after a blinding heavenly flash (something young boys enjoy and horsemen and dogs hate), ends with the Lord's charge to seek doctrinal instruction quick.[1]

But Luke's famous tale is fond fiction, cadging details from popular healer lore. It is the conversion of gentile believers at Luke's church that his story actually portrays, overwriting Paul's own mystical reminiscence, which expressly rules out the picturesque and doctrinaire. Luke hopes his Greek readers will recognize the fish scales (*lepídes*) falling from Paul's eyes after catechism. A healing legend from the book Tobit, which those Greek readers would know, describes the prophet's son Tobias grinding up a whole fish, pasting it over his father's blind eyes to dry, then peeling off a thick cataract film. Here

Luke's embellishment adds medical wonder, showing how the new technique of cataract treatment was held in popular awe, with religious associations.[2]

Paul never refers to Luke's Damascus script, however, and he was dead for a decade before Luke wrote it. Paul's known letters invoke light as a salvific metaphor exclusively, never hinting at hazard or injury.[3] When he mentions stumbling blocks, he compares converts' former blindness with newly healed vision. By contrast, describing his own dramatic transformation, Paul speaks of new hearing, not sight. Some commentators bypass Paul's own tale as inscrutable private mysticism; but in fact its terms dominate his final letter to Rome, which we study here. His crucial words appear in italics below, and we shall return to them. Far from a "conversion," that prophetic call more deeply reinforced Paul's lifelong Jewish faith.

Saying #71 • *What Paul Heard*
It is necessary to boast; nothing is to be gained by it, but I will go on to visions and revelations of the Lord. I know a person in Christ who fourteen years ago was caught up to the third heaven—whether in the body or out of the body I do not know; God knows. And I know that such a person—whether in the body or out of the body I do not know; God knows—was caught up into Paradise and *heard words said that no human being is allowed to chatter.* —2 Cor 12:1–4

BRINGING YOUR CORNER

- *Did you come by your religious ideas by sudden insight, or over years?*
- *Did one person inspire you? Or community experience? Or private reading?*
- *Did others ask you about it? Was it easy or hard to answer?*

D. HOW WORDS MATTER

If language is not correct,
then what is said is not what is meant.
If what is said is not what is meant,
then what must be done remains undone.
If this remains undone,
then morals and art will deteriorate.
If justice goes astray,
the people will stand about in helpless confusion.
Hence there must be no arbitrariness in what is said.
This matters above everything.
—Confucius[1]

There is no such thing as *mere* language. Linguist Noam Chomsky writes: "Language is not for communication; communication is easy without it. Language is for *thought.*" Philosopher Martin Heidegger writes pithily, "Language is the house of being." The Book of Genesis opens with God's first creative deed, which is speech.

Saying #71 • The Creation
When God started making the heavens and the earth,
the earth was a lifeless mass awash in a dark sea, with a
wind—God what a wind it was!—roiling the waters,
and God SAID 'Let light BE,' and Light WAS. —*Genesis
1.1*

Words dominate Genesis further. In the second chapter
(actually invoking an earlier legend), Adam's first job is *naming*
the creatures: that is how God reckons that Adam needs a
helpmate, and from his rib creates Eve, who converses *verbally*
with the serpent.[2] The Patriarch Abram receives a new *name*,
Abraham, with promises *spoken* first—circumcision
commanded only later in his ninetieth year.[3] Moses is also
called by *name* first of all, before learning God's plan.[4]

PART EIGHT
HOW PAUL ARGUES IN ROMANS

Paul left us a dozen letters to congregations he had founded or knew, engaging basic issues that shape every human community. At the same time, they express his faith with winning prose that has comforted Christians ever since. Most missives reprove strife and plead for peace and love. Nonetheless for that, this one letter to the church at Rome actually aroused later conflict.

The Letter to the Romans gives us a rare glimpse of Paul's full-crafted logical design. Unlike the patchwork of Paul's other letters on urgent topics, the Roman letter interweaves many biblical ideas into an extended fabric. Whereas Jesus' fragmented teachings pulled bright thematic threads from the prophets, Paul embraced the prophets' far-spreading thought patterns and added colors from Genesis for a coherent carpet design.

Here as elsewhere, Paul asserts the primacy of salvific faith above following rules: a question that still vexes believers today. Since the European middle ages, diverse interpretations of that letter have separated Western church denominations. Reform and renewal movements have borne banners quoting it, while they marched with idealistic hope toward new Christian unity. This author's belief that Jesus and Paul do meet at a meaningful corner inspires him to join that march.

The claim that Jesus was risen, which Paul had initially opposed, undercut other Jewish reform agendas. Nonetheless, he never disowns his famed teacher Gamaliel or other rabbis who taught him; on the contrary, he boasts they succeeded.[1] In his earlier letters, Paul naturally invoked the common image of a divine courtroom, where God judges everyone's ethical performance.

Moreover, non-rabbinical reformers like John Baptist weighed performance just as heavily. Jesus' connection with the Baptist is doubtful, however,[2] and Paul never mentions him. In my earlier book, *Signs of Life* (2019), I proposed that we read the Jordan Baptism story as a passion meditation, like the Transfiguration story, and I showed that iconographers East and West have long linked the two that way.[3]

Meanwhile from his own hard secular experience, Paul decided that our courtroom chatter misrepresents God's active relations with humankind. Luke's Book of Acts retells how religious rivalry filled Mediterranean town life with debates, public uproar, and magistrate proceedings. Preaching to pagan crowds, Paul stirred that civic pot wherever he went.

Around the Mediterranean he founded local convert churches (Greek *ekklêsiai*), and suffered arrest, beating and jailing many times. Finally, Luke tells how Paul's birth at Levantine Tarsus had lent him the threadbare cloak of Roman citizenship, which he donned at last by appealing above a local magistrate to Caesar's tribunal at the capital. Then traveling for trial, he wrote Roman Christians—all evangelized by his fellow Jews—an apology for his career among the unclean gentiles.

Jews were used to legal talk, and Hebrew scripture enjoins judges to put wrongs right, exacting public restitution where possible. Moreover, Roman civil law assures open procedure. It is no wonder then that Paul opens his Roman letter with commonplace law court imagery, a homiletic habit from his early writings. Only now, after Paul's career of courtroom encounters, does his Roman letter overwrite that with very different talk drawn afresh from Hebrew scripture.

BRINGING YOUR CORNER

- *Who are your heroes in sport or family duty or politics?*
- *What makes Perry Mason and Law & Order popular TV courtroom dramas?*

A. A REVOLUTIONARY
APPROACH

Beginning after World War II, scholars have emphasized the sturdy Jewish fiber that runs throughout Paul's writings. He believes God's ancient promises distinguish Jews forever.[1] Born Jews have always lived by faith that God would fulfill those promises. Paul credits that faith as their constant motive: in Abraham's long journey, in Moses' revelations and leadership, in the endurance of later exiles—and supremely in Jesus' life and death.

By comparison, very few first century Jews acknowledged personal conversion, a practice of pagan cults.[2] Some rabbis welcomed gentiles' faith, but none allowed them membership in the chosen people, entrusted with God's promises to Abraham. Most teachers recognized religious identity by birth alone. Like skin color, it could never change or be changed. The circumcision ritual that Jews shared with Philistines and Egyptians had no tribal value, since "gentile impurity was not ritual impurity, and could not be cleansed. We have no evidence that any author or editor whose work the Hebrew Bible preserves perceived [circumcision] to be a rite of entrance into the Israelite nation, for there was no such rite."[3]

Unlike some other missionaries, Paul opposed circumcising gentile converts, not as needless, but as fruitless. Jews like himself—and he was proud to be one—were born to inherit, and were God's chosen forever. Gentile converts could only be adopted instead. Though foreigners could not become Jews to inherit those promises, Paul knew gentiles might share their Hebrew faith. His unique calling was to carry foreigners the good news that God had fulfilled promises entrusted to Jews, and had spread Jesus' faithful Spirit abroad, so that the whole adopted human race might now reap them.

Adoption was Paul's Revolution. Hebrew scripture nowhere mentions adoption; indeed, Paul's idea differs from the blessing that young families cherish today. Although death then took nearly half the children born, and many of their mothers too, polygamy (marrying many wives) and Levirate (marrying a late brother's widow) supplied backup heirs to Jewish maternal lines. But Greco-Roman families, like others worldwide, might legally adopt grown males with skills for carrying a patriarch's clan heritage onward.

Adoption was always Grace: a free gift to candidates who had no proper claim upon it. A few adopted heirs had natural siblings also, who shared that heritage. Most adult adoptions were replacements, however—an implication that Jewish Paul loyally ruled out in Romans 9-13. (In some Asian countries today, adoptees take on lifelong legal responsibilities also, largely replacing those they had inherited at birth.) Instead, Paul lifts a horticultural metaphor from other rabbis: grafting, where two plants maintain their separate genetic fruits, and may even be separated or recycled again.[4] So although circumcision creates an advantage for Jews, it makes no difference in moral responsibility. What counts for Jews and foreigners alike is Faith.

BRINGING YOUR CORNER

- *Are you or any relations or friends adopted? Would you volunteer your experience?* (Their experience is private; do not ask for or share theirs!)
- *Is your worship life your own inheritance, or did you take on a different tradition?*

Paul's Roman letter offers a natural place for the long carpet border of his thoughts to form a corner juncture with Jesus' tighter woven edge. Jesus worked in Galilee, a northern province with native Jewish government (but answering to Rome), and preached to his own people, addressing a non-Jew but four times in the gospels.

By contrast, the letter to the Romans is Paul's sole communication addressed to fellow Jews[5]—some possibly circumcised as adults, contrary to Mosaic law[6]—yet wishing to be called Jews. Here he readies our loom for braiding both teachers' borders together where they meet, the way many traditional carpet corners do. In earlier letters to foreign churches he had founded, Paul urged converts to follow his cherished Jewish ethics. Writing to Galatian Christians, for example, Paul recites centuries of Jews' faith in God's promises, and demands converts behave like their adoptive fellows.

But he has never visited Rome, where he may die (Paul did) and presumes community members there learned about Jesus from Jews who had known him (Paul had not) and will share religious Jews' dismay at immoral gentile society. So here he anticipates Jewish objections to his argument about faith's equal potency for all.

Paul's reasoning won over at least some believers, who spread his missionary scheme as churches grew by conversion. One might say the first Jews who accepted foreign members are called Christians. Not many centuries later, non-Christian Jews would allow for foreigners' conversion as Christians did.

BRINGING YOUR CORNER

- *What other religious traditions do you know personally?*
- *What about your family's doctors, teachers, cleaners, and safe guardians?*
- *Do you welcome and reward Helpers equally from all nations and classes?*
- *Should Christians teach their children about other faiths?*

Various Bible prophetic books do speak about God's favors to foreigners, promising that Jews will share worldwide blessing and peace with them. Yet Paul never appeals to those prophecies in his Roman apology, perhaps because he hunts bigger game along an older and higher mountain trail.

His own story of his transformation points the way: "caught up to the third heaven," he "heard words said that no human dares to chatter."[7] Paul's quarry is the role words play

in bounding human thought. For empty human chatter, Paul
uses the Greek verb *laléo*, babbling—"blah blah blah." Job's
comforters practice it too.[8] Likewise, Buddhists warn that our
"chattering minds" impede enlightenment.

Well-trained in pharisaic legal study and informed by his
own many brushes with secular courts and jails, Paul resolved
that legal court speech only conceals humankind's true relationship with God. In his Roman letter, Paul set out to replace
chatter about God as a magistrate with the language of faith.
Twelve centuries earlier, he anticipated Thomas Aquinas: "I
cannot believe that God is a Judge."

B. A COMMON PUZZLE: BIBLE LOGIC

P aul's reasoning in Romans may stump some interpreters, but he follows scriptural convention. Hebrew scripture is filled with debates, very often quoting both sides. For one celebrated example:

> *Saying #72 • Answering Fools*
> Do not answer fools according to their folly, or you will be a fool yourself. Answer fools according to their folly, or they will be wise in their own eyes. —*Prov 26:4-5*

We have noted how Hebrew editors rarely erased earlier theology, but overwrote it with their own.[1] That is why modern fundamentalists can still flaunt harsh threats that the Bible's Hebrew editors actually meant to flood and flush away.

Hebrew scripture recounts two debates that Paul's Roman Jewish readers knew well. In one, Abraham bargains with God to spare the city of Sodom.[2] Pressed steadily to cut the number of righteous men God requires to spare the city, YHWH finally agrees that if Abraham can find just ten righteous men there,

God will spare the whole city—but he cannot, and Sodom is destroyed. Elsewhere, Moses bargains with God to spare the Israelites who worshipped a golden calf.[3] After first proposing to destroy and replace them all from Moses' progeny, this time God relents in order to preserve the divine reputation.

Some modern readers hear those stories as Human Heroes Changing God's Mind—but the Hebrew editors meant no such thing! They likely chose a well-known *halakah* story-form because their new theology was controversial. Pagan cults knew nothing like it. So they borrowed familiar rug-bargaining dialog to underscore how forgiving YHWH always and constantly is. Both stories emphasize YHWH's royal *praüs* virtue, holding to long-term benign purpose and never distracted by anger.[4] Every rug-collector knows that is how real rugs are traded.

Rug dealing does not make enemies. Rhetorical questions, where the questioner already knows the answer, typify biblical revelation of YHWH, and appear in gospels too. For example: *Ma li w'lach/lachem?* ("What is that to you and me?" meaning always "This is God's business, not ours!") just before David, Elijah or Jesus work saving wonders.[5] "Whose image is on the coin?" "What does the Law command you to do?" "Are you envious because I am generous?" "Am I not to take pity on the city of Nineveh?" "A king? Who told you that?"

Jewish synagogues expect such argument to this day. First the rabbi tells believers what they ought to do; then the believers answer by telling the rabbi why she is wrong. That is Jews' traditional theological duty, loftier than unquestioning obedience.

BRINGING YOUR CORNER

- *What are your news sources?*
- *Do they differ or agree? Do they challenge or reconfirm your opinions?*
- *How has it turned out they were wise?*
- *If you already know what they will say, why consult them?*

C. ANOTHER COMMON PUZZLE: PAUL'S LOGIC

P aul's rhetoric likewise summons up discordant rationales. A famous apocryphal seminarian, challenged on exams to explain this final letter, wrote: "The argument in the Letter to the Romans can be explained by the fact that St Paul had two heads, one of which kept shouting 'God forbid!' to what the other said." But the Roman letter actually moves on one steady course, the way planets circle the sun, while Paul reckons his readers must follow him. Only one of those "heads" speaking is his own.

Medieval philosophers argued by logical syllogisms, a rhetorical form the Spanish Arab Ibn Rushd (Latin name Averroes) and Neapolitan Thomas Aquinas perfected just sixty years apart.[1] Syllogisms draw a two-dimensional straight line: if a=b, and b=c, then logically also a=c. Twelve hundred years before them, however, Paul reasoned more like an astronomer watching the planets.

All the planets travel around our sun in the same direction, but because of the way its orbit overlaps Earth's, the planet which ancient Chinese astronomers named Water-Star

(*Shŭixīng*), and Europeans Mercury, appears to cycle backward ("retrograde") across our sky three times yearly. Paul's contemporaries watched every other visible planet—Venus, Mars, Jupiter, Saturn, and Uranus—back up by slower rhythms. Indeed, the Greek word "planet" means "wanderer."[2]

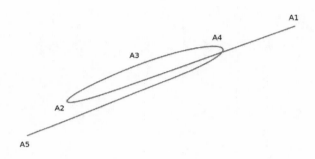

For example, Mars seemed to take this illusory looping path across our sky in 2009-2010, while actually moving steadily forward around the sun, along with our Earth.

Likewise, Paul's Roman letter periodically revisits points he made earlier, so that his readers must match up those looping overlaps to track his real advance. We will take the liberty of tying those logical loops the way a carpet weaver might do, but a line-by-line commentator hardly can. For example, Paul's ten repeated protests "God forbid!" loop back, closing off retrogressions to law court argument, which Paul steadily means to supplant.[3]

Sayings #73–82 • TABLE OF PAUL'S TEN LOOPED PROTESTS: *Mê génoito / God forbid!*

	God Forbid!	Paul's Rebuttal
Romans 3:3–4	*Will their faithlessness nullify the faithfulness of God?*	Though everyone is a liar let God be proved true.
Romans 3:5–6	*Is it unjust of God to bring retribution on us?*	How else could God judge the world?
Romans 3:31	*Do we overthrow the law by this Faith?*	On the contrary, we uphold the Law.
Romans 6:1–2	*Are we to continue in sin that grace may the more abound?*	Baptized into death, we cannot sin in future.
Romans 6:15–16	*Should we sin because we are not under the law, but under Grace?*	We were slaves to sin, but now we are enrolled in free obedience to God.
Romans 7:6–7	*Dare we say that the law is sin?*	No, but without having known what it is to covet, I would not have coveted.
Romans 7:12–13	*Did what is good (= the law) bring death to me?*	Sin, working through what is good, brought death and Sin beyond measure.
Romans 9:14–15	*Is there injustice on God's part?*	God declares freely: I will have mercy on whom I will have mercy.
Romans 11:1–2	*Has God rejected his people?*	There is a remnant chosen by Grace.
Romans 11:11	*Have they (= the Jews) stumbled so as to fall?*	Their stumbling brought salvation to gentiles.

The palette of rebuttals in the right-hand column incorporates one color that Paul's Jewish readers will welcome: all ten are painted with scriptural orthodoxy. Like a bright-hued planet orbiting across the heavens, however it may seem to wander, Paul's trajectory holds steadily traditional. He never claims to replace the "old" Testament with something new or better. Not even his revolutionary idea of adoption lessens the Jews' advantage in receiving God's oracles. Not even his beacon of love dims the Mosaic Law's elaborate ethic.[4] Ritual purity and moral purity have one common source there.

And yet one debate pattern, customary elsewhere, is missing—a significant fabric gap. Those left-hand protests vary randomly, as if arising in some open public market; but Paul's right-hand rebuttals are linked to show one method woven throughout. Paul will not answer a fool according to his folly—see Saying #69, above—so the courtroom manipulations implied by protests on the left here are not answered in kind. For example, "Are we to continue in sin that grace may the more abound?" proposes a clever lawyerly trap. But instead of taking that bait, Paul invokes death, the destroyer of all chicanery. Other protests win answers quashing their implications too. If God judges the world, as the prophets say, God yet remains utterly free to punish or forgive, as no human judge would be. Hence the casuist's presumptive courtroom is rejected, leaving no chance for coercing God. On Tavistock terms, the boundary between God's power and our human will stands still secure. The courtroom and its judge must give way to a different vision, which Paul will claim means living by Faith.

D. A THIRD COMMON PUZZLE: PAUL'S OTHER HEAD

The apocryphal student fantasy that Paul had two heads points up a singular problem: more than other letters, understanding Romans requires tracking his duple rhetoric. One head speaking in those *Mê Génoito* loops (on the chart's right) is plainly Paul's own. Whose then is the apparent other head?

In his letters to gentile congregations he founded, Paul responds to real adversaries (unnamed)—who boost circumcision, for example—dismissively, much the way a politician might do. By contrast, his *Mê Génoito* rebuttals in Romans avoid ridicule, a favorite Pauline tactic elsewhere.[1] It seems this "other head" is not a typical rival.

We do know other dialogic forms. As mentioned before, the rug dealer does not battle. Abraham and Moses bargain with God in the same way. Here Paul assumes educated hearers and means to befriend and win them over. Paul's "other head" speaks for his readers—seasoned Jews in his day; now, you and me.

More like an *Aikidō* martial arts master than the Roman
gladiators Paul drew on for metaphor in earlier letters to
gentile churches, [2] Paul's *Mê Génoito* rebuttals show adversaries working almost as partners to welcome and turn challenges to long-term advantage.

No other New Testament letter boasts such a list of rational
ripostes. Individually one or another may seem defensive, but
read together those ten rejoinders conjure potential friendliness the way Abraham's and Moses' prayers did, and Adam
should have done when God questioned him like a friend who
had come to walk with him in the garden. Now as we speak up
through Paul's "other head," you and I learn to hear his
friendly good news. [3]

BRINGING YOUR CORNER

- *Has anyone ever changed your opinion on something
  you had thought was plainly obvious?*
- *Have you made friends with a rival?*
- *Have you trained a beginner to do something they
  thought at first would never feel natural?*

While tying together so many ideas distributed around this
Roman letter, I hope the reader will sense Paul's Hebraic warp
underlying throughout. On the other hand, his logical weft
loops make this textile assembly cumbersome to print up
simply, the way we quoted Jesus' parables, each straight
through. And whereas we studied Jesus' parable fragments in
our own editorial order of rising confrontation, Paul's final

letter obliges us to trace his original reasoned linkage, joining the dialog as he invites his Roman readers to do. My verse-numbered footnotes here will reveal how I have bound his long threads into related knots like a classic carpet. I encourage my readers in turn to confirm or propose better combinations.

E. A FOURTH COMMON PUZZLE: THE HUMAN ANIMAL

One repeated weaver's snag is Paul's Greek word *sarx*, rendered *"flesh"* in classic dictionaries, and so in Latin and Jacobean English Bibles. But Rabbinic Hebrew underlies Paul's Greek.[1] In Hebrew, *Yetzer ha-tov*, impulses for the Good, labels our ethical life. The contrasting *Yetzer ha-raq* (Paul's *sarx*) does not mean impulses for evil however, but rather our animal nature.

As one rabbi wrote, "Without *yetzer ha-raq*, no man would marry, build a house, or follow a career." Just so. Paul's *sarx* labels the natural impulses we humans share with other animals: aggression, nesting, building, related affection, and yearning for offspring, for example. *Yetzer ha-tov* adds ethical goals, thereby bringing humans lifelong existential struggle. Recent biologists say other animals have also evolved impulses toward self-sacrifice, and even toward collaboration between species rather than ruthless competition.[2] Nonetheless, even though animals do not know the Law and so cannot sin, psalmists and rabbis reckoned that animal nature and unenlightened human *yetzer ha-raq* (Paul's *sarx*) lead alike to death.[3]

Yetser ha-tov and Yetser ha-raq collaborate:
Zookeeper Mary Wilson grooms cheetah Laika.
(Photograph by Richard Stacks, Baltimore Sun.)

BRINGING YOUR CORNER

- *Should we protect or shoot wildcats that attack runners on forest trails? What if the zoos are already full?*
- *What do we do about wild animals that people take as pets, but that express native violence suddenly? (Chimpanzees are notorious for that change.)*
- *How do we respond when a human acts unethically, but out of deep animal nature?*

Unlike us, of course, animals are "dumb"—that is, they cannot speak. This recalls the gift that underlies Paul's own story of his transformation, when he "heard words said that no human dares to chatter." Just so in Romans 8, the Spirit translates prayers that our animal desires do not know how to say. The human mystery lives beyond words.

In contrast to chattering minds, shared *silence* is where mystery lives: a cherished skill we learn to perfect through long practice on retreats, and briefer silences together in worship. St. Gregory Nyssen parish services hold a full minute of silence after every scripture reading, welcoming God to speak to the congregation.

BRINGING YOUR CORNER

- *Do you enjoy rising early and sitting by yourself? Sitting together silently in church?*
- *Meditating?*
- *Walking by yourself? Cycling or swimming? Cooking alone? Reading?*
- *Have you made a silent retreat? What happened?*

Back to the opening of Romans. Before revealing his new language of faith, Paul astutely invokes familiar courtroom imagery for a standard rabbinical diatribe against paganism, which his Jewish hearers will recognize.[4] Pagan myths assume a proper hard boundary between mortals and the immortal gods. But Gentiles blur that boundary, hoping to gain a godlike happy life. They worship idols that are mere statues of humans, or attack the boundary for sex, producing demigods like Hercules. Whereas in Jesus, Paul finds a healthy and enduring boundary relationship linking God and humankind.

In Jewish law courts "the punishment fits the crime" exactly. Inasmuch as pagans swap the true God for human idols, says Paul, they don't know what it is to be human, so they do inhuman things and applaud those in the coliseum and theatre.[5] Thus God has "given up" (condemned) pagans to their own desires, as any first century rabbi might tell you.

Paul argues much as Amos did, that the Jewish attempt to manipulate the boundary between God and humankind will earn us a similar fate.[6] Dysfunction around boundaries is a favorite Tavistock research focus, and here is Paul's expert diagnosis: All Jews know that God has kindness, patience, and tolerance, as well as great power.[7] Joel 2:13 spells that out clearly, and the Hebrew editors reprinted Joel's words many times throughout their scriptures.[8] Nonetheless even we Jews do not respond with gratitude and change our life plans, the way the prophet begs us to do. Instead, like pagans we switch God's character role from Joel's patient friend into a judge who rewards performance.

Jesus' parable of the pharisee and the tax collector makes this very point.[9] This pharisee obeys more than Moses' law demands, and he pretends to thank God—when covertly he seeks recognition for his own ethical performance, which will make him more powerful. He believes in lies that doom him ("I am not like other people"), whereas the real God showers sun and rain upon righteous and unrighteous farmers alike.[10] The tax collector tells just two truths: he is a sinner, offering no pledge to reform, and yet God has strong *chesed* love for him.

The Pharisee's performance-judge God is a lie; the Tax

collector's Faith in God's *chesed* love is true. So the truthful Tax Collector goes home put right with God, while the self-deceived Pharisee does not.

BRINGING YOUR CORNER

- *Is telling the truth hard sometimes? In this discussion group, for instance?*
- *Have you been surprised by opponents who listened to you?*
- *Have you changed your opinion in response to their listening?*

F. OUR RELIGIOUS "NEEDS"

Much the way Jesus enacted Isaiah's and Joel's ancient prophecies, Paul draws upon the Book of Genesis. God opens Genesis chapter 3 by coming to walk companionably through the garden with Adam in the cool of the day. Missing Adam's company, God speaks four questions that a true friend (unlike the guileful serpent) might ask. "Where are you?" "Who told you that you were naked?" "Have you eaten the fruit I told you not to eat?" "Why did you do that?"[1]

Adam's answers dodge responsibility, and so elicit new commands from God—but not changed intentions. From there onward God offers friendship nevertheless. Not even sin can frustrate God's design. Why then does our common screenplay costume God as a judge?

Sociologist of religion Peter Berger reckons that humans worldwide harbor one basic "religious need": someone should keep the universe stable for them. We can add to this a moral corollary: somehow the universe should care that we are right. Being right is not a satisfaction in itself; we need it to *make a difference* that *we* are right. Both of these are control demands. Neither Jesus nor Paul honors them, however.[2]

Control makes for rules rather than creativity. Jesus' parable protagonists are notoriously bad at keeping sound rules—like fairness, honesty, or even a respectably tidy house. No wonder unstable, creative Vincent Van Gogh sold only two paintings during his lifetime, in contrast with well-behaved, rule-following academic artist contemporaries. Likewise, academic science today reckons religious belief outmoded, and rules out mystery. Nevertheless Nobel geneticist Francis Collins writes: "The more I examine the universe and the details of its architecture, the more evidence I find that the universe in some sense must have known we were coming."[3] Today's astronomers seek reliable "laws" in universal action— even though some "laws" still lack concrete proof.

BRINGING YOUR CORNER

- *Have you served as umpire during a game?*
- *Have you had to declare who was right when you weren't certain?*
- *When the crowd calls "Kill the Umpire!" do you sympathize? With whom? And why?*

PART NINE
PAUL'S FRIENDLY GOD

In place of rules we can manipulate, Paul argues for living by faith. As he reads scripture, faith is what has always counted for Jews. God uttered promises to Abraham long before any command to circumcise, for example.[1] And Jesus simply returned to Abraham's example, by living out his Faith in God until he gave up his life. So God raised Jesus and spread his spirit everywhere, and in baptism all share his victory over death.[2]

Never arguing for what reward might be due them, Abraham and Jesus said "Thank You" to God. And so can we. Hence Sin was no problem for Abraham—a question that worried rabbis reading Genesis chapter 20, where a cowardly Abraham lies sacrilegiously about his marriage to Sarah, nearly dooming their host Abimelech and his whole household. (Gentile Abimelech still welcomes Abraham graciously upon learning the truth.) Thus Paul insists that Abraham's Faith sufficed to overwhelm even deadly wrongdoing, because God is faithful even if humans are not.[3]

God talks with Moses as a man talks with his friend, and gives him friendly-God instructions, much as God originally gave to Adam in the Garden.[4] Don't kill each other or steal, society cannot work that way. Respect your parents: when you become a parent in turn, you'll be glad you did. As Paul reasons, the Law itself—whether from Jewish Moses or pagan Hellenized conscience—is "holy and just and good" for our common lives.[5]

Knowing that laws come from a trustworthy friend provides the firmest footing for obedience. Ideally, we would do the right thing out of gratitude, not fear of a judge, but no one responds gratefully.[6] That is why God gives Moses the "holy, just and good" written Law,[7] so that from our predictable failures,[8] we humans will recognize our sin—that is, our resistance to the true relationship between God and ourselves.[9]

BRINGING YOUR CORNER

- *Has a friend ever pulled you back from making a big mistake?*
- *Has a friend's shared experience saved you trouble?*
- *Has a friend guided you someplace new?*

A. WHAT IS SIN?

Saying #83 • Doing Something Extra for God
Woe to you...hypocrites! For you tithe mint, dill, and
cumin, and have neglected the weightier matters of the
law: justice and mercy and faith." —*Matt 23.23*

Both gentile conscience and Mosaic law fail because
there is *in us* something they cannot handle. To identify it, Paul evokes the first and best-known biblical
example.[1] In Genesis 3, Adam and Eve covet God's knowledge
of Good and Evil. At the serpent's guileful prompt, they grasp
for something they actually already have: namely, being like
God. As Genesis put it earlier, "Let us make humanity in our
image and likeness"[2]

Their coveting, not ignorance, makes the essential difference. Paul sees his fellow Jews likewise coveting God's power
—a central Tavistock theme[3]—as an illusory moral advantage
beckons them.

Christian readers might overvalue the pharisee's hollow
claim in Jesus' parable: "I fast twice in the week, and pay

tithes on all I possess," unaware both boasts exceed the kindly commandments of God's Torah. Ironically, those mention no fasting, and tax certain crops only—never herbs like mint, dill, and cumin—and merchants and rabbis such as him not at all. It was a common teaching by rabbis in Jesus' time that mercy and justice outweigh all observances, however motivated.

Hidden human motivation is the real scandal here. Doing extra seductively suggests ethical control, as if to say, "God, you are so nice I'd like to make a contribution," or "I don't want you to help me win, I want to win myself." Thus we humans would mask our anger at the boundary separating us from God.[4]

Like all their descendants, once Adam and Eve disobey because they covet God's power, they hide themselves. "Where are you?" "Who told you you were naked?"[5] Concealment pervades human experience. Psychoanalyst and Yale School of Medicine professor Stanley Leavy writes: "Concealment is not just episodic, like lying or other forms of conscious dissimulation. It is habitual, literally characteristic."[6]

Psychology Today magazine says the average North American tells hundreds of lies every day. "Lovely to see you." "I'm doing great, thanks." "I'll be there in a minute." Even self-deception is comfortable for us—a trait that depth psychology explores, and salespeople depend upon. As Jacobean High Chancellor Francis Bacon writes, "The mixture of a lie doth ever add pleasure."[7]

Hence in Genesis 3, God sets the first enmity within creation: between Adam and the serpent, between human obedience and lies. That difference is why John's Passion has Jesus reply to Pilate, "A King? *Who told you that? You may talk such stuff, but* I was born to witness for the truth." Muslims too believe that Jesus always speaks the truth. Islam preserves several traditions we used to share, including speech later lost from Christian writings.[8]

BRINGING YOUR CORNER

- *When is it easier to lie? Better to lie?*
- *Have you found ways to talk with people you strongly disagree with?*
- *Do you and your family know topics you never discuss?*

A secret covetous desire to control our relationship with God motivates our obedience to the Law.[9] Here is the Sin which enters and kills me through the good law, making me subject to judgment instead of God's promises. Even as we plan clever moves to manipulate the Judge, Sin crouches in our doorway like a predator awaiting a foolish passerby to devour.[10] So my experience of the Law is that someone else (Sin) lives in my house, doing things I hate,[11] and instead of spelling out God's promises, the Law becomes a condemnation experience. Naturally, suffering follows—the target of Buddhists and Freudians alike. Leavy writes:

> The root of neurotic pain lies in the fact that all sufferers distort their desires out of the basic human incapacity to fulfill them. To put it in simplest form: because we cannot always have what we want, we pretend to ourselves that we want something else. As I have said, the effectiveness of psychoanalytic treatment is based on that assumption: through the discourse, the dialogue, the sufferer penetrates

his own disguises, speaks his desires. That does not guarantee their fulfillment, but it frees him of their distortions.
Freud's wry comment that psychoanalysis changes neurotic
suffering into ordinary misery may not sound too hopeful,
but it is a candid appraisal of man's fate.[12]

BRINGING YOUR CORNER

- *Have you desired something you were told you should
  not desire? What did you pursue instead?*
- *When did you rediscover your first desire?*
- *Have you done something you wanted, before you got
  permission or support?*
- *What later support did you get?*

Paul insists that the Law is salvific for human life, yet humans
misuse it dangerously.[13] This writer once served as a Yale
freshman advisor to a roomful of young women including a
diagnosed psychopath, unable to learn right from wrong. That
student had been warned that if she could not live with others,
she would lose her college place. But because she could never
internalize others' reactions, when taking food from the
common refrigerator for example, she lived in terror of
violating normal social customs and broke down in tears
whenever she did so. In turn, her roommates lived in constant
anxiety for her, and had to restrain her daily from ruin.

BRINGING YOUR CORNER

- *What does holding someone accountable mean?*
- *Have you spoken up at a town or school board meeting?*
- *What has talk of institutional "reform from within" meant for you? Is it real?*
- *The same court verdict brings widely different sentences in Norway, USA, and China. Whose justice is that?*

Unlike a courtroom judge, the true God gives steadfast *chesed* love freely, whether to just or unjust people, Jew or gentile.[14] Abraham simply believed, and God counted his Faith as rightness.[15] In the same way, you might imagine a golf professional telling you, "Yeah, that's a golf swing, we can work with that," when you know you have a long way to go.

After all, this is the kind of God who makes the dead live and brings into being things that don't exist yet.[16] So making faith stand in serving in place of rightness is child's play for God. Once giving Moses the law that exposes sin, for aeons God allowed sin to pile up, so that God could impress upon us how easily sin can be forgiven.[17] Jesuit poet George MacCauley likens this strategy to the magician Harry Houdini, who piled on chains and locks to emphasize how easy were his amazing escapes.

BRINGING YOUR CORNER

- *Tell your experience learning (1) a musical instrument or (2) a sport or (3) a language.*

- *Does coaching a sport differ from playing it? Which satisfies you more?*
- *Does teaching art differ from creating? What is art appreciation?*

Because we don't like living with a friendly God and want to control the relationship, we invent a judge-God—but end up instead as "slaves to sin,"[18] relinquishing the moral freedom we had under the true, faith-based system. That is precisely The Sin. We "feel guilty": a desperate attempt to keep control —not responsibility but control.[19]

Paul does not warn us against factual guilt—"I actually ran the stop sign"—but manipulative guilt—"My mother is the East Coast distributor for guilt." Thus we try to control God's forgiveness, or even punish God for providing it. The terminal human grasp for control is suicide—in its way, a desperate survival mechanism. Rapid intervention psychologists like the famous Richard Fisch redirect that very drive for control into changing suicidal behavior.[20]

BRINGING YOUR CORNER

- *Have you seen fine organizations defeat their own chosen high purpose?*
- *Why do committees fight instead of working together as they supposedly agree to do?*
- *Have you ever held an impossible job?*

B. GOD'S FREEDOM

Invoking the gospels' repeated preference for creating forgiveness above receiving it, McCauley summarizes the Roman letter's ethic: God is committed to absolution, and so must we be.[1]

Paul's letter insists that both Moses' Law and the gentile conscience remain "holy and just and good" for every nation's life.[2] Six of his ten "God forbid!" protests insist upon that. Each objection earns a response declaring God's true nature and quashing Sin.

Saying #84 • Sin Exposed
It was sin, working death in me through what is good,
in order that sin might be shown to be sin, and through
the commandment might become sinful beyond
measure. —*Rom 7:12-13*

These protests echo the Hebrew prophets' timeless concern: "How else could God judge the world?"[3] The grace received through Jesus' life and death affords us no free pass back to sin; instead, it recommits us to justice and rightness.[4] God is not a judge we can manipulate, because God remains free to punish wrongs or pardon them, unlimited by courtroom protocol.[5]

God's freedom to punish or pardon we call "poetic justice" ("It serves them right!") and historians have recorded it often enough. Confucian political philosophy has upheld it for millennia, and it surfaces in voters' talk with every democratic election. By terrible contrast, armed vigilantes settling old scores cast bloody shadows on "just revenge." We can only hope for God's steadfast *chesed* love to end retributive justice. Instead our own past century has seen genocide, ethnic cleansing, economic repression, exceptionalism and "alternative facts." All these intensify our hope for the right future—once acquittal, reparations or forgiveness seal our history. That is why the prophets call us to change plans, and Paul appeals for new commitment to God's friendly laws. Recent scholarship likewise rediscovers Jesus' express honor for the revealed Law, including the Mosaic commandments for ritual purity.[6] Among their contemporaries, Jesus and Paul were law-abiding Jews. Rather than hasten an apocalyptic end, both teachers urge their nation and all humankind to respond afresh and live.

BRINGING YOUR CORNER

- *Evidence for the genocide and enslavement of Indigenous peoples and the lynching of free blacks are well established. At what age do you want school children to know of them?*

- *Today Indigenous peoples are still North America's poorest ethnic group. What is to be done now?*

C. GOD'S ANSWER TO SIN

Now we can watch Paul bind together his logical loops like carpet knots. At last God has put an end to sin—and to our covert, manipulative Judge-talk. Jesus' death was effective through his faith and God's faithfulness. (McCauley warns Calvinists: Note that here Paul denies their judicatory language of redemption.)[1] By hanging on a tree Jesus broke the Mosaic law[2] but God is faithful and raised Jesus from the dead nonetheless, pouring out his Spirit on the world, and so making his death a life-giving sacrifice.

Our imaginary God—the Judge—implies that one sin by Adam brought us the condemnation of Death. Nevertheless, after our long history of sin, the true friendly God has made us righteous on account of Jesus' faith.[3] Even if some remain faithless, God has strong, faithful *chesed* love, so a *baruch* outcome is secure.[4] The opposite blend, with a faithless God, would have been lethal. But God has no interest in condemning creatures.

So if you must still think legalistically, God has done something in Jesus that cut sin's timeless chain to death. That boundary between God and humankind, which we humans are so covetous about, God has erased by becoming human and dying for the unrighteous.[5] In Tavistock terms, that wipes away both sources of people's anger: the false perception that they are separate from God; and their felt need for "being right."[6]

Jesus stayed faithful unto death, and Paul assures us that all Christians inherit Jesus' victorious rewards as they receive his Spirit at baptism.[7] Thiessen reckons Christ's *pneuma* transforms foreigners thus into Abraham's promised seed: here lies the brilliance of Paul's revolutionary concept of Adoption. Far from setting Jesus' followers apart from other faithful peoples, Baptism unites humanity by joining adopted gentiles to God's promises—which Jews like Paul have been forever guaranteed to receive.[8]

BRINGING YOUR CORNER

- *Where have you found good causes to serve that you did not recognize at first?*
- *Where have you found allies that you did not expect?*
- *What changed your mind?*

Paul's earlier letter to the Philippians spells out this core theological argument, drawing on his favorite Hebrew scripture, Genesis, and notably lacking courtroom imagery.

Saying #85 • Christ Emptied Himself
Let this same mind be in you that was in Christ Jesus,

Who though he was in the form of God *[like Adam
and Eve]*
Did not regard equality with God
Something to be seized, *[as Adam and Eve did]*
But emptied himself,
Taking the form of a slave,
Being born in human likeness *[as Adam and Eve were]*.
And being found in human form,
He humbled himself *[as Adam and Eve did not]*,
And became obedient to the point of death—*[which
Adam and Eve shared because of their disobedience]*. —Phil
2:6-8

Here psychoanalyst Stanley Leavy finds God's remedy for
concealment in particular.

To sharpen the Christian relevance of this psychological
picture, I would like to consider the supreme act of unconcealment: the historical event of God's life with us on earth, as we
understand it in the life of Jesus, and its sequel in his avail-
ability to us all the time. At the heart of the Christian Faith is
the revelation of the hidden One, the unseen Creator of all that
exists—including our minds—who has worked within the
evolving fabric of existence since the beginning and made
himself known in Jesus.[9]

Both these arguments prove Christ's incarnation salvific in
itself, thus sidestepping the Western Christian quicksand of
substitutionary atonement. By contrast, Paul warns that those
who live by animal nature (*sarx*) still live by the law and sin
and death, not recognizing what sort of God they are dealing
with.[10] Leavy concurs:

Every bit of fresh understanding that we gain of the created
universe is a new evidence of God's unconcealment, as is

every new insight into the meaning of Christ's incarnate life. We can never grasp or understand that life in its fullness. Mankind, even in the Christian dispensation, can neither stand nor understand this reality and tries again and again to conceal the redeeming Presence beneath all-too-human vestments, making out of our infinitely loving God a very human creature of power, pride, rage, and riches.[11]

BRINGING YOUR CORNER

St. Teresa of Ávila, fleeing Spanish Inquisition soldiers with her nuns, was overturned in a highway ditch and cried, *¡Señor, si así tratas a tus amigos, por supuesto son pocos!* "Lord, if this is how you treat your friends, no wonder they are few!"

- *Has life given you fair cause for anger at God?*
- *How about the world news?*
- *To whom have you expressed your anger?*

D. PRAYER THAT WORKS

Replacing courtroom chatter with faith, Paul changes our spiritual talk altogether. In Jesus Christ we learn a new grammar, one that is life-dealing, not death-dealing: spiritual laws worked out in the Spirit who has plumbed the depths of God and knows who God really is. [1]

The children of God are those who live no longer by gentile conscience or Jewish law alone, but by God's system of promises, so we can cry "ABBA, Father." [2] We now have only the first fruits of this growth towards being children of God. We hope for it. Its full fruiting will impact the physical universe as well. [3]

Meanwhile, however, our prayer remains manipulative prayer, because that is how we learned to control powerful people (parents, teachers, guardians) when we were children. Behavior guru Werner Erhard argued that the most effective way to manipulate people is ...

E. GET A GUN

Our usual prayer method is to get a gun and train it on God, as follows.

God, give me a bicycle and I'll be good.
God, I love you, now give me a bicycle.
God, thank you for all your past gifts. Now give me a bicycle.
God, I admit I am not worthy. Now give me a bicycle.
God, help me to make my whole life perfect so that I may deserve a bicycle.
God, purge my heart of every manipulative thought, so that it will be truly appropriate for you to give me a bicycle.

That is your author's whole prayer life. Do you have any other prayers?

Pulling a gun on friends can hardly succeed for long, as most of us learn. We don't know how to pray to a friendly God who loves Jew and gentile alike, the perfect God who shines with no shadow of turning one way or another.[1] We don't even have the vocabulary.[2] In Romans 8, Paul uses the same Greek verb *laléo,* recalling his own transformation when he heard words that no human dare chatter—blah blah blah.[3] But the Spirit fills us, translating for us—the Spirit who knows God and has plumbed the depths of God[4] —because God is faithful and won't ultimately let us fall away.

> *Saying #86 • No Separation from God*
> I am convinced that neither death, nor life, nor angels,
> nor rulers, nor things present, nor things to come, nor
> powers, nor height, nor depth, nor anything else in all
> creation, will be able to separate us from the love
> (*chesed*) of God in Jesus Christ. —*Rom 8:38-39*

In earlier letters to gentile churches he had founded, Paul referenced Greek Hellenistic speculation about high cosmic powers vying over human life. But in this letter, addressed to believing Jews, those powers scarcely appear—not even in his anti-pagan diatribe at Romans 1. Pagan idols and sophisticated pagan religion alike lack life for Paul.

The later New Testament Book of Revelation , with its heavenly war, is yet to be written. Nor have the third century's metaphysical Persian visions appeared, claimed by "Mani, a follower of Jesus Christ." Those would become Augustine's first engagement with Christian belief.[5] Unlike all such speculations, in Paul's last letter Abraham, Moses, David, Jesus and Paul are all mortal men—some of them legendary perhaps, but none cosmic contestants. God's incarnation holds steadfastly monotheist, following the Hebrew principle that grants God only one friend or enemy: our human race.

BRINGING YOUR CORNER

- *Have you ever ignored advice from a parent or lover, and then found the advice was right?*
- *Whom did you tell afterward?*

F. JOINED IN FUTURE

The following chapters of this Roman letter insist again that God's promises to Jews are secure forever, and Jews will ultimately rejoin with gentiles in a permanent faithful body. Writing near his own life's end, Paul hopes those Jews who did not recognize Jesus, and so missed their first chance, will one day resume their rightful inheritance. Such risk was a consistent theme in Jesus' parables, though Paul never quotes those. Paul pictures the Jewish return like grafting a fallen branch back onto Faith's olive tree.[1] (Warning to Christian supersessionists, who suppose the Church might supersede Judaism! In horticulture, a grafted branch bears its native fruit without conversion.)

So after weaving and knotting his rhetorical carpet, sometimes looping his threads in seeming retrograde, Paul ties them off where the risen Jesus awaits him: at God's faithful friendship with humankind. Cannot this truth be the words Paul heard spoken in the third heaven years before, which no human dare chatter about, but only accept with thanks?[2]

Paul expounds love more explicitly than Jesus' parables do.

Hence modern readers can welcome Confucius' advice, that "saying what is meant matters above everything."[3] Paul's celebrated paean to love in 1 Corinthians, while read today at countless weddings, points well beyond romantic bonds.[4] Simon May observes that idealizing marital love is peculiar to our recent era, and may no longer hold.[5] Indeed, Paul's first Corinthian letter advocates his own practical celibacy.[6] His lyrical love paean rather describes God's gift to the human community at large, manifest in all human friendship. Echoing his own prophetic call, Paul begins by winnowing his speech the way ancient Chinese Confucius and modern British linguistic philosophers alike urge.[7]

Saying #87 • Love Extolled

If I speak in the tongues of mortals and of angels, but do not have love, I am a noisy gong or a clanging cymbal. And if I have prophetic powers, and understand all mysteries and all knowledge, and if I have all faith, so as to remove mountains, but do not have love, I am nothing. If I give away all my possessions, and if I hand over my body so that I may boast, but do not have love, I gain nothing. Love is patient; love is kind; love is not envious or boastful or arrogant [5]or rude. It does not insist on its own way; it is not irritable or resentful; it does not rejoice in wrongdoing, but rejoices in the truth. It bears all things, believes all things, hopes all things, endures all things. Love never ends. And now faith, hope, and love abide, these three; and the greatest of these is love. —*1 Cor 13*

Here is not the abstracted *agapê* that Christian preachers assembled two centuries later, salvaging the choicest lumber from the common feelings stockpile that Paul and his readers knew.[8] Hebrew scriptures and raw community experience together shaped Paul's concrete moral structure. His architecture of endurance and forgiveness undergirds all loves human and divine, and he relies upon that foundation beyond even Faith and Hope.[9]

BRINGING YOUR CORNER

- *Have you ever started out in one direction and then changed paths?*
- *Have you seen someone change their life for the better? How did their original character and potential still show up?*

PART TEN
FRIENDSHIP FOLDS IT ALL TOGETHER

学而时习之，不亦说乎？
有朋自远方来，不亦楽乎？

Is it not a pleasure studying long and hard?
Is it not a pleasure having friends come from afar?
—*The opening couplet of Confucius'* Analects, *5ᵗʰ century BCE*

We have been hunting for the point where Jesus' and Paul's teachings meet, though Jesus and Paul never did. Without quoting each other, they left us similar woven edge-patterns framing life's whole polychrome carpet. We combed Jesus' parables for recurring telltale threads; we analyzed Paul's rhetoric for harmonious design. A decade after Paul had died, John's gospeler wrote: "No one has greater love than this, to lay down one's life for one's friends."[1] Although neither Jesus nor Paul coined those words; nonetheless both their life stories meet easily at this common corner.

Projecting human experience onto God's actions gives us

all our theological language. As Confucius' metaphors might have it, the purpose of our long and hard study is friendly shared work, like folding a carpet. And God's friendship marks the corner where Jesus' terse stories and Paul's far-stretching thoughts braid together.

Friendship is a worldwide human trait, evolved to advance our species' survival. Yale sociologist Nicholas Christakis observes that unlike kinship, friendship opens alliances between un-related un-equals, where tit-for-tat reciprocation is neither required, nor sometimes even possible.[2] Such was the relationship Hebrew YHWH had meant to have with Adam and Eve;[3] and when they broke it, YHWH awarded it uniquely to Moses.[4] Again unlike kinsfolk, Christakis discovers that human friends experience themselves as un-substitutable, un-replaceable, special, and trusted. Such experiences define friendship within every culture. Some social animals (elephants, chimpanzees, whales) also exhibit like behavior. It would appear that the historical evolution of friendship first made conscious individuals real. Without friendship, we would be mere gene pool hordes, like swarming spiders and wasps.

BRINGING YOUR CORNER

- *Have you befriended someone you disliked or envied at first?*
- *Have you traveled with someone who became a longtime friend?*
- *Have you been surprised by someone's friendship?*

Among humans, this behavior is supremely ancient. A gift for friendliness is likely how *homo sapiens sapiens* outlasted the Neanderthal and every other hominid, because our forebears evolved to collaborate better, and so survived the last Ice Age. As anthropologists summarize, "Being best connected is better than being strongest."[5] Indeed, Darwin's evolutionary idea triumphed during his lifetime thanks to his own gift for making friends among colleagues like Thomas Huxley and South American Christian ministers, both Catholic and Protestant.[6] Risking one's life (or life career) to aid a non-relative is our species' distinctive behavior,[7] one that Jesus the healer taught by example.

No wonder then, that Gregory of Nyssa closed his final book, *The Life of Moses,* exhorting us to seek perfection by becoming God's friend.

Saying #89 • *Becoming God's Friend*

These things concerning the perfect virtuous life...we have written briefly for you, tracing the life of the great Moses in outline like a pattern of beauty, so that each one of us might copy the beautiful image shown to us by imitating his way of life. What more trustworthy witness that Moses did attain the perfection which was possible would be found than the divine voice which said to him: *I have known you more than all others?* It is also shown in the fact that he is named the "friend of God" by God himself, and that [Moses,] by preferring to perish with all the rest if the Divine One did not through his good will forgive their errors, stayed God's wrath against the Israelites [worshipping the Golden Calf]. God averted his judgment so as not to grieve his friend. All such things are a clear testimony and demonstration of the fact that the life of Moses did ascend the highest mount of perfection...

It is time for you to look to that example, and transferring it to your own life, be known by God and become God's friend. This is true perfection: not to avoid a wicked life because like slaves we servilely fear punishment, nor to do good because we hope for rewards, as if cashing in on the virtuous life by some business deal. On the contrary, disregarding all those things we do hope for, and have been promised us, we regard falling from God's friendship as the only thing dreadful and we consider becoming God's friend the only thing truly worthwhile. This as I have said, is the perfection of life.

Alongside Jesus' own authentic stories and sayings, we have seen how the gospels repeat his teaching within a choir of harmonic voices. Far from compromising his innovative thought, such collaboration is a unique human skill. Our discussion as we read this book exemplifies it.

Shared singing even precedes speech, and so is older than every language.[8] Singing together happens worldwide and binds friends like nothing else. During the COVID pandemic many church congregations—encouraged to worship safely but not to sing—broke their silence despite the political price. At secular musical performances, too, the audience plays a crucial creative role.[9]

Saying #90 • Crowd Collaboration
Here's one thing that I've learned that's relevant to churches. I learned that what really makes a rock show is the crowd. A great band helps the crowd to figure out how to *be* the show. You can't have a great rock show if

you're only one person seeing the greatest rock band. It's just not going to be what rock and roll is supposed to be. So many churches say: we've got to give them a great show, with the best music, and blow them away, and send them home with the best preaching, and the best coffee and all of that stuff. Well, I think that's missing the point: the really most amazing things that can happen at church can come out of the congregation. I discovered this at St. Gregory's, when I noticed that the beauty of the sermons was actually a collaboration. The preacher would preach, and then a moment of silence, and then people would stand up and share their own experiences that came to mind during the sermon—not that their experiences proved more interesting, but the experiences allowed me to see the size of what had been discussed. —Jacob Slichter, rock drummer, *Semisonic*

BRINGING YOUR CORNER

- *Do team sports differ from individual sports? What about concert playing?*
- *When could you really start speaking a new language?*
- *Have career or family changes increased your friendships? Do your new friends mix with the old ones?*

Jesus and Paul each overcame human resistance to God's reign, rebutting our maneuvers for control while we vainly tried to mask our motives. Both teachers drew upon millennia of

Hebrew theology—law and prophets combined. Above all, by trusting in God's promises and laying down his life for his friends, Jesus revealed the rug's knotted apex point—the same corner where he and Paul meet in our Bibles, though they never met in their time. Confucius teaches every era to lift up that one corner they make, so the whole world can bring back the rest of life, and fold together God's bridal carpet of love for us to store.

APPENDIX
HOW TO PLAY THE GAME "JESUS ON YOUR TELEPHONE"

Choose eight to ten volunteers. (A flipchart easel or whiteboard and markers are convenient, but not necessary.) Tell everyone that we will deliver a saying by Jesus to one another in turn, each time explaining what we believe it means. Excuse all volunteers except one from this room to a nearby place acoustically separate.

Write on the flipchart or whiteboard: "BE YE APPROVED MONEYCHANGERS." Show this saying to the volunteer and say: "The saying is actually from Jesus, though quoted in an ancient writing outside our Bible." Ask if there are any questions, and let the volunteer memorize it. Cover or hide the saying from view. Instruct those in the room to respond approvingly to anything they hear recited or explained. Rehearse with them once.

Invite the second volunteer into the room. Explain: "You will now hear the tradition, and what it means." Let the first volunteer recite the tradition and explain it to the second volunteer. (Be sure to have them explain it.) Ask the second volunteer: "Does this remind you of other sayings or stories about Jesus?" Ask: "Do you have any questions? You record what they say on the flipchart or another pad. Let the second volunteer sit down.

Cover or hide from view what you wrote with the second volunteer. Remind the group to respond approvingly to whatever they hear.

Invite the third volunteer into the room. Explain: "You will now hear the tradition, and what it means." Let the second volunteer recite the saying and explain it. (Be sure they explain it.) Ask the third volunteer: "Does this remind you of other sayings, or stories about Jesus?" Ask: "Have you any questions?" Record what they say on the flip-chart or another pad. Let the third volunteer sit down, and summon the fourth.

Repeat the dialog process with each volunteer until the last volunteer has received the tradition. Invite the last volunteer to tell the group the saying, and what it means to them. Ask the group: "Have you any questions?" Let the last volunteer answer.

Uncover or show the original saying, "BE YE APPROVED MONEYCHANGERS." Read out the changes in the saying and the group's interpretations. Promise them we will study this saying together shortly, and what it means.

WORKS CITED

Ames, Roger T. and Rosemont, Henry Jr. *The Analects of Confucius: a Philosophical Translation* (New York: Ballantine, 1998).

Augustine. *Confessions* (5th cent. CE)

Bacon, Francis. "Of Truth," *Essays*, 1625.

Berger, Peter L. *The Sacred Canopy: Elements of a Sociological Theory of Religion* (Garden City: Doubleday, 1967).

Birnbaum, Philip. *A Book of Jewish Concepts,* (New York: Hebrew, rev. 1975).

Breech, James. *The Silence of Jesus: the Authentic Voice of the Historical Man* (Philadelphia: Fortress, 1983).

de Marneffe, Daphne. *Maternal Desire* (New York: Little, Brown, 2010).

Brown, Raymond, SS. *The Community of the Beloved Disciple: The Life, Loves, and Hates of an Individual Church in New Testament Times* (New York: Paulist, 1979).

— "The Gospel according to John," *Anchor Bible* (Garden City: Doubleday, 1966).

Christakis, Nicholas A. *Blueprint: the Evolutionary Origins of a Good Society* (New York: Little, Brown Spark, 2019).

Collins, Francis S. *The Language of God: A Scientist Presents Evidence for Belief* (New York: Simon & Schuster Free Press, 2006).

Confucius. *Analects* (5th cent BCE): see trans Ames, Roger T., and Rosemont, Henry jr (1998) and Ware, James (1980).

De Vaux, Roland. *Ancient Israel, Its Life and Institutions* (London: Darton, Longman & Todd, 1961).

Fabian, Rick. *Signs of Life: Worship for a Just and Loving People* (New York: Church Publishing, 2019).

Freud, Sigmund. "The future prospects of psycho-analytic therapy," Opening Address at Nuremberg, 1910. *Complete Psychological Works of Sigmund Freud*, Standard edition, vol. x, p. 146 (London: Hogarth, 1957).

Fuller, Reginald H. *The Foundations of New Testament Christology* (New York: Scribners, 1965).

Funk, Robert *et al. The Five Gospels: The Search for the Authentic Words of Jesus* (New York: Macmillan, 1993).

Green, H. Benedict, CR. *The Gospel According to Matthew* (Oxford, 1975). (CR = Community of the Resurrection at Mirfield, Yorkshire, UK.)

— *Matthew, Poet of the Beatitudes* (Sheffield, 2001).

Gregory of Nyssa: *The Life of Moses*, A. Malherbe and E. Ferguson, trans. (New York: Paulist, 1978).

Hare , Brian & Woods, Vanessa. "Survival of the Friendliest," *Scientific American* (August, 2020) p.58.

Hart, David Bentley. *That All Shall Be Saved* (New Haven: Yale 2019).

Jeremias, Joachim. *The Parables of Jesus,* 8th ed. (New York: Scribners, 1970, 1972).

Jeremias, Joachim. *The Unknown Sayings of Jesus* (London: SPCK, 1957, 1964).

Kittel, Gerhard, and Friedrich, Gerhard. *Theological Dictionary of the New Testament,* trans. Geoffrey Bromiley, German abbr. *TWNT* (Grand Rapids: Eerdmans, 1964-1976).

Koenig, John. *The Feast of the World's Redemption: Eucharistic Origins and Christian Mission* (Harrisburg: Trinity, 2000).

Lathrop, Gordon. *Holy Ground: a Liturgical Cosmology* (Minneapolis: Fortress Press, 2003).

Leavy, Stanley A. *In the Image of God: a Psychoanalyst's View* (New Haven: Yale, 1988).

MacCauley, George SJ. *The Truce of God* (Denville: Dimension, 1972).

— *The God of the Group* (Niles: Argus, 1975).

MacMullen, Ramsay. *The Second Church: Popular Christianity A.D. 200-400* (Atlanta: Society of Biblical Literature, 2009).

May, Simon. *Love: a History* (New Haven: Yale, 2011).

— *Love: a New Understanding of an Ancient Emotion* (Oxford, 2019).

McCullough, Michael. *Beyond Revenge: the Evolution of the Forgiveness Instinct* (San Francisco: Jossey-Bass, 2008).

Musil, Robert. "Die Amsel" (1936), *Sämtliche Erzählungen* (Hamburg: Rowohlt, 1957).

Nock, Arthur Darby. *Conversion: The Old and the New in Religion from Alexander the Great to Augustine of Hippo* (Oxford: Oxford University Press, 1933).

Nodet, Étienne and Taylor, Justin. *The Origins of Christianity: An Exploration* (Collegeville: Liturgical Press, 1998).

O'Loughlin, Thomas. "The Eucharist as 'The Meal That Should Be'," *Worship* 80 (No. 1, January, 2006).

Patton, John. *Is Human Forgiveness Possible? A Pastoral Care Perspective* (Nashville: Abingdon, 1985).

Paul, Shalom M. *Amos: A Commentary on the Book of Amos* (Hermeneia) (Minneapolis: Augsburg Fortress, 1991).

Perrin, Norman. *Rediscovering the Teaching of Jesus* (London: SCM, 1967).

Poliakoff, Michael B. *Combat Sports in the Ancient World: Competition, Violence and Culture* (New Haven: Yale, 1987).

Prudlo, Donald S. *Thomas Aquinas: A Historical, Theological, and Environmental Portrait* (New York: Paulist, 2020).

Reynold Lewis, Katherine. *The Good News About Bad Behavior: Why Kids Are Less Disciplined Than Ever—And What to Do About It* (New York: Hachette Public Affairs, 2018).

Roughgarden, Joan. *Evolution's Rainbow: Diversity, Gender and Sexuality in Nature and People* (Berkeley: University of California Press, 2004).

Sapolsky, Robert. *Behave: the Biology of Humans at our Best and Worst* (New York: Penguin, 2017).

Saritoprak, Zeki. "Who is Jesus for Muslims?" *The Christian Century,* June 2, 2017, pp. 32-34.

Schell, Patience A. *The Sociable Sciences: Darwin and His Contemporaries in Chile* (New York: Palgrave Macmillan, 2013) p. 6-7.

Spinney, Laura. "How Farmers Conquered Europe," *Scientific American,* July 2020, pp. 60-67.

Stendahl, Krister. *Paul among Jews and Gentiles* (Philadelphia: Fortress, 1976).

Thiessen, Matthew. *Contesting Conversion: Genealogy, Circumcision and Identity in Ancient Judaism and Christianity* (Oxford 2011).

— *Jesus and the Forces of Death, the Gospels' Portrayal of Ritual Impurity within First Century Judaism* (Grand Rapids: Baker Academic, 2020).

— *Paul and the Gentile Problem,* (Oxford: 2016).

Thurman, Howard. *Jesus and the Disinherited,* (Boston: Beacon 1976).

Tomlinson, Gary. *A Million Years of Music:* (New York: Zone, 2015), ch. ii., iv.

van Kamm, Adrian. *Envy and Originality* (Garden City: Doubleday, 1972), pp. 21-23.

Vermès, Geza. *Jesus the Jew* (New York: Macmillan, 1973).

Ware, James R. *The Sayings of Confucius* (New York: Mentor Religious Classics, New American, 1955, 1980).

Wiesehöfer, Joseph. *Ancient Persia from 550 BC to 650 AD,* Azizeh Azodi, trans., second edition (London: I.B.Tauris, 2001 & 2011).

Yoder, John Howard. *The Politics of Jesus* (Grand Rapids: Eerdmans, 1972).

Zamoyski, Adam. *Napoleon: a Life* (New York: Basic Books, 2018).

NOTES

INTRODUCTION

1. Analects 15.28.

LIFTING UP ONE CORNER

1. R Donald Prudlo, "Thomas Aquinas was a failure," *Thomas Aquinas: A Historical, Theological, and Environmental Portrait*, 2020, p.301. Prudlo judges that Thomas Aquinas' lifelong project planting Aristotle atop Christian theology did not succeed. Today many times more people know Confucius. Watching my own labors at his classical tongue, one fellow seminarian challenged: "Why do you want to speak Chinese?" My simple defense: "Most people do."
2. Confucius, *Analects* 7:8, fifth Century BCE. Harvard scholar Achilles Fang reads thus the classical fifth-tone character *fuk* "to fold," enduring typically in today's second tone *fú*. Unlike other readers' fourth-tone *fù*, "I will not repeat myself," Fang keeps the original metaphor.

HEARING DIFFERENT TUNES AT ONCE

1. Judges 16. The Greek Septuagint translation (labeled LXX for its seventy legendary translators) borrows this term to render diverse Hebrew names for love, perhaps avoiding the Greek *eros*. Among those names, Hebrew *ahavah* is uniquely unreasoning, with no imitable virtue. In proper theological use: "How odd of God to choose the Jews;" or Prussian Chancellor Otto von Bismarck's "Divine Providence shows special care for fools, drunkards, and the United States of America."
2. 1 Corinthians 13.
3. Galatians 5:12.

HOW BOTH ECHO THE BIBLE

1. Matthew Thiessen, *Jesus and the Forces of Death* (2020); *Paul and the Gentile Problem* (2016).
2. The Amalekites in 1 Samuel 15.

3. 1 Kings 18, 2 Kings 5:1-19
4. For two centuries Israel's royal Bethel shrine had revered the historical Golden Calf among other polytheist images (1 Kings 12, 2 Kings 10). But once Amos prophesied there (745+ BCE) under southern Kings Hezekiah and Josiah, YHWH became Judah's sole world deity, and a consistently reliable moral actor. Hebrew editors intruded that theological innovation throughout their scriptures. Hence Jesus' parables, Paul's arguments, and Mohammed's prophecies all assume it. It cements their three lineages today more strongly than Abrahamic myths ever could.
5. See Part 8, below.

I. JESUS SPEAKS FOR HIMSELF

1. Howard Thurman, *Jesus and the Disinherited*, pp. 79-80.

A. CATCHING JESUS' OWN VOICE

1. James Breech, *The Silence of Jesus: the Authentic Voice of the Historical Man*, (1983) p. 4
2. H. Benedict Green, CR, *The Gospel according to Matthew* (1975). *Matthew, Poet of the Beatitudes* (2001). CR: the monastic Community of the Resurrection at Mirfield, West Yorkshire, UK.
3. The rich field of context criticism shows early churches faithfully at work shaping the scripture to fit their emerging theology. This warrants proper study on its own—but that lies beyond this book's scope.
4. Étienne Nodet and Justin Taylor, *The Origins of Christianity: An Exploration*, (1998) ch II. Examining all gospel evidence outside the Jordan Baptism story, these historians conclude that Jesus and the Baptist never actually met.
5. Luke 23.41-43.
6. For example, 2 Thessalonians 1:7, 2:3. Romans 2:5. Mark 8:38-9:2 // Matthew 16:27-28 // Luke 17:30-31. Matthew 13:41. The World's End also fills a book styled Revelation or Apocalypse, but that was the last book bound into our Bibles and Eastern Christians never read it in church.
7. Reginald Fuller, Norman Perrin, Geza Vermès, among many others. Frederick Borsch lamented to me that these so swiftly reversed a century's critical agreement, sidelining his own deep study of Jesus' "Messianic Consciousness." That split still divides commentators today.

B. THE SIGN OF THE WELCOMING TABLE

1. Luke 15:2 "This guy welcomes sinners and dines with them." *"Houtos hamartolous prosdekhetai kai synsethêei autois."* *Houtos* (= *this one*) used alone is dismissive.
2. Luke 15:2. John Koenig. *The Feast of the World's Redemption: Eucharistic Origins and Christian Mission,* (2000), ch. 1. Gordon Lathrop, *Holy Ground: A Liturgical Cosmology* (2003), pp 64-65. Thomas O'Loughlin, "The Eucharist as 'The Meal That Should Be,'" *Worship* 80 (No. 1, January 2006).
3. Isaiah 25:6-8, quoted above.
4. John 15:13-15.

A. ECSTATIC RESPONSE TO GOD

1. This book follows NRSV translations except where historical critics modify our received text. Among many others: Robert Funk, *Parables and Presence* (1983) and *The Five Gospels* (1993); Joachim Jeremias, *The Parables of Jesus,* 1954, 1972; Norman Perrin, *Rediscovering the Teaching of Jesus,* 1967; Geza Vermès, *Jesus the Jew,* 1973. Alterations to the NRSV text appear here in *italics* throughout.
2. Simon May, *Love: a New Understanding of an Ancient Emotion,* (2019), Part 4.
3. Augustine, *Confessions,* Book I.
4. Katherine Reynold Lewis, *The Good News about Bad Behavior: Why Kids Are Less Disciplined than Ever—and What to Do about It,* 2018, offers ten pages of select bibliography.
5. Karen Horney, "Flight from Womanhood" (1926), cited in Daphne de Marneffe, *Maternal Desire* (New York: Little, Brown 2010), pp 62-63.
6. See Matthew Thiessen, *Jesus and the Forces of Death: the Gospels' Portrayal of Ritual Impurity within First Century Judaism* (2020).

B. WHAT YOU NEED AND NEEDN'T KNOW

1. The books of Proverbs, Ecclesiastes, Wisdom, and Sirach (Ecclesiasticus).
2. Laura Spinney, "How Farmers Conquered Europe," *Scientific American,* July 2020, pp. 60-67.

C. WHEN WE CANNOT KNOW

1. Jonah 4:11.

D. ASTUTE RESPONDERS

1. At Acts 10:34, Peter congratulates a pagan centurion: *Ep' alêtheias katalambanomai hoti ouk estin prosôpolêmptês o theos.* Commonplace cult believed riches and power were marks of a god's favor: see similar reproofs at Colossians 3:25, Romans 2:11, Ephesians 6:9, James 2:1, 1 Peter 1:17.
2. J.Jeremias, *Unknown Sayings of Jesus* (1957), cites Clement of Alexandria among many other sources.

A. CUNNING RESPONDERS

1. Adrian van Kamm, *Envy and Originality,* (1972), pp. 21-23. See Part 6, below.
2. Mark 15:10 // Matthew 27:18.
3. Joachim Jeremias, *The Parables of Jesus,* 1958. Norman Perrin, *Rediscovering the Teaching of Jesus,* (1967) pp. 94-98.

C. FOOLISH RESPONDERS

1. These two are essentially the same Psalm.
2. John 7:49.
3. Exodus 12:15,19; Deuteronomy 16:4. R. De Vaux, *Ancient Israel: Its Life and Institutions* (1961) ch. 17.
4. The gospel of Thomas (96:1-2) trims details, including the high poundage, and reinterprets leaven as a small doughball that yields big loaves. Contrasting small-against-big typifies Thomas' re-editing of other parables too. (Funk et al., *The Five Gospels,* p. 523.) Jesus' seed parables do picture desirable growth in numbers, but on the scale of a home kitchen three full measures (fifty pounds) of leaven make an unusable disaster.
5. The *Oxford English Dictionary* records this non-monetary moral meaning first in 1526.
6. Romans 1:18-32.

D. LESSONS IN SELF-DESTRUCTION

1. Joachim Jeremias *The Parables of Jesus,* 1954, 1972. Geza Vermès, *Jesus the Jew,* 1973.

E. IMPORTUNITY

1. Mark 8:33 // Matthew 16:23.
2. John 18:34, 37.
3. Luke 15:2.

F. CONTRARIAN SAYINGS—ICONOCLASM

1. Matthew Thiessen, *Jesus and the Forces of Death,* ch. 5.
2. Find a close paraphrase inserted at Exodus 32:12-14, 34:6-7, and Numbers 14:18 and 15:11. And stamped atop older threats of endless punishment at Exodus 20:6, Deuteronomy 5:10-12, and 7:9-10. RSV editor Robert Dentan identified twelve citations within the Pentateuch plus allusions in Psalms and other prophets.
3. Thiessen, *Jesus and the Forces of Death,* ch. 7.
4. Luke 19:1-10.

G. THE BEATITUDES

1. Captain Dennis Holahan, USN.

H. FLINTY SAYINGS & SAMARITANS

1. Matthew 5:4. The word *praüs* is a bisyllable, pronounced *pra-EES* in Biblical and modern Greek alike.
2. Wiesehöfer, Joseph, *Ancient Persia from 550 BC to 650 AD,* (2001 & 2011), p.33.
3. Isaiah 50:7. Thanks to Bishop William Swing for this prophetic connection.
4. Matthew 11:29-30. In the Bible's agricultural talk, "yoke" means farm work, not slavery; and "heart" is where we make plans, not experience feelings. See the *praüs* monarchs at Ecclesiasticus 45:4, and in Gregory of Nyssa's third Beatitude sermon.
5. A few marginal variants of Lk 23:34a call for forgiveness as well, and many popular Bibles print those texts.
6. Zeki Saritoprak, "Who is Jesus for Muslims?" *The Christian Century,* June 2, 2017, pp. 32-34.
7. Matthew Thiessen, *Jesus and the Forces of Death,* Ch. 7, "Jesus, healing, and the Sabbath life."
8. Amos 5:18.
9. See the Samaritan woman's complaint in John 4. Raymond Brown links that gospel with Samaritan Christians.
10. Jeremias, *The Parables of Jesus,* p. 204.

11. Greek has just two simple verbs for "see" whereas English has dozens, most very distinctive like "eying" and "glimpsing." In this story, "eying" fits naturally, and suggests inner tension rather than instinctive fear.
12. Greek *hêmithanê*, lit. "half dead."
13. Thiessen, *Jesus and the Forces of Death,* pp. 115-116, cites Leviticus 21:1-3, and contemporary use of Deuteronomy 21:23. See Tobit 1:17-19, 2:3-9, 12:12-14.
14. Raymond E. Brown SS, *The Community of the Beloved Disciple: The Life, Loves, and Hates of an Individual Church in New Testament Times* (1979).

IV. JESUS SPEAKS AMONG FRIENDS

1. Matthew Thiessen, *Jesus and the Forces of Death* (2020).

A. THE CORONA IN OUR DARK SKY: GOD'S LOVE FOR THE POOR

1. Robert Sapolsky, *Behave: the Biology of Humans at our Best and Worst,* (2017).
2. Mark 10:21 // Matthew 19:21 // Luke 18:21

C. BAR MAAJAN AND LAZARUS

1. Jeremias, *The Parables of Jesus,* pp. 182-187, outlines a long folk tradition behind this parable, retelling reversals of fortune in the afterlife. The spare details in Jesus' story imply that his hearers know several versions well enough already.
2. Leviticus 19:31. Hence Saul's doom upon asking the Endor witch to quiz the late prophet Samuel. 1 Samuel 28.

D. THE JUBILEE AND LORD'S PRAYER

1. John Howard Yoder, *The Politics of Jesus,* (1972).

E. ALREADY FORGIVEN

1. Exodus 16.
2. Michael McCullough, *Beyond Revenge: The Evolution of the Forgiveness Instinct,* (2008).
3. John Patton, *Is Human Forgiveness Possible? A Pastoral Care Perspective,* (Nashville: Abingdon 1985)

4. Shakespeare, *The Winter's Tale*, 1623; Calderón de la Barca, *La Vida es Sueño (Life is a Dream)*, 1635.
5. Lk 23:34a
6. Mt 5:39-41 // Lk 6:27-30
7. John Patton, *Is Human Forgiveness Possible? A Pastoral Care Perspective*, (1985) p. 176. Italics original.

G. FAITH IN GOSPEL STORIES

1. Syrophoenician woman at Matthew 15:28. Gentile noble at Mark 8:10 // Luke 7:1. Paralytic's friends at Mark 2:5. Bleeding woman and Jairus' daughter at Mark 5: 34,36. Bind man at Mark 10:52.
2. The Samaritan leper at Luke 17:19.
3. Simon Peter at Matthew 16:17.
4. Mark 13:28, Luke 12:29.

H. THE GREAT ASSIZE TRIBUNAL

1. David Bentley Hart, *That All Shall Be Saved* (2019).
2. Luke 18.1-5.

I. LOVE'S SCANDAL

1. John 15.13.
2. Parable 25, above: Mt 25.14-28 // Lk 19.12-25.
3. The *Oxford English Dictionary* records this non-monetary moral meaning earliest in 1526.
4. Hebrew *mikshol/makshelah* and Greek *skándalon* or *próskomma*—these occur interchangeably.
5. Leviticus 19:14. Such cruel pranks typified the mockery pervading biblical laughter, long normative until Roman satirists Plautus and Terence created the kinder comedy we know.
6. Jeremiah 6:21.
7. See 1 Corinthians 1:23, 8:9. Romans 9:32-33, 11:9. Revelation 2:14.
8. Gordon Lathrop, *Holy Ground: A Liturgical Cosmology* (Minneapolis: Fortress Press 2003) 64f. Cited also in Thomas O'Loughlin, "The Eucharist as 'The Meal That Should Be'" *Worship* 80 (No. 1, January 2006).
9. Matthew 11:6 // Luke 7:23 in Greek: *makarios estin hos ean mê skandalisthêi en emoi*.

A. JESUS' BEST PUPILS THEN AND NOW

1. Mark 1:30 // Matthew 8:14 // Luke 4:38.
2. H. Chadwick, *Jerusalem and Rome*, Fortress Press 1964.
3. Matthew 21:31-32. Luke 15:2. John 7:49.
4. Mark 5:25-34.
5. Thiessen, *Jesus and the Forces of Death*, ch. 4.
6. Matthew 11:12 // Luke 16:16.
7. Luke 11:5-8 and 18:1-5.
8. Luke 15:11-32.
9. Luke 10:38-42.
10. Luke 10:42. *Mariam gar tin agathin meridan exelegato.* The "good part."
11. Mark 10:15 // Luke 18:17.
12. Matthew 20:1-16.
13. John 8:3-11. See Matthew 7:1-5 // Luke 6:37-42.
14. Mark 7:25-30 // Matthew 15:22-28. Her bold riposte to Jesus is almost always mistranslated. The affirmative *naí* was always emphatic in Hellenistic Greek, and the conjunction *gar* always means "because"—never "but," as most English versions would twist it. She is not pleading for an exception but bluntly debunking bad logic—and thereby commonplace opinion.
15. Romans 2:11, 3:29-32.
16. Mark 16:1-8 // Matthew 28:1-8 // Luke 24:1-12, 22-24 // John 20:1-18. Thomas lacks Resurrection tales.
17. Romans 4:17.

B. PAUL'S CHRISTIAN WOMEN FRIENDS

1. 1 Corinthians 7:5-9.
2. 1 Corinthians 7:5-9. 14:33-35.
3. 1 Corinthians 16:19. Romans 16:3, 13, 15. Colossians 4:15.

VI. JESUS' AUTHORITY

1. The questioner was Dr Stephen Holtzman, your author's husband.
2. Amos 1:3-2:16.
3. Amos 7:10-17.

A. GROUP LIFE: TAVISTOCK

1. Adam Zamoyski, *Napoleon: A Life* (New York: Basic Books 2018), p.459.
2. Sigmund Freud, "The Future Prospects of Psychoanalytic Therapy," Opening Address at Nuremberg, 1910. *Complete Psychological Works of Sigmund Freud*, Standard edition, vol. x, p. 146. (London: Hogarth 1957). Italics mine. Thanks to psychologist Dr Jonathan Dunn for this quotation.
3. Mark 11:27–33; Matthew 21:23–32; Luke 20:1–8; see also John 6:40–47.
4. Thiessen, *Jesus and the Forces of Death* (2020), pp.113-119.
5. Amos 5:21-24.
6. Thiessen, *Jesus and the Forces of Death* (2020).
7. Especially John 17.
8. Raymond Brown, SS, *The Community of the Beloved Disciple,* (1979) *The Gospel according to John,* Anchor Bible, (Garden City: Doubleday 1966).
9. Matthew Thiessen, *Jesus and the Forces of Death,* p. 6; ch.4
10. Mark 2:5–11. Geza Vermès shows the expression "Son of Man" (*bar nash*) is an Aramaic circumlocution for "I" or "a human like me. *Jesus the Jew,* ch. 7.

B. KNOWING AN ORIGINAL MAN WHEN YOU SEE ONE

1. John 18:34 & 37
2. The Ethiopian Tewodros Othodox Church numbers Pilate and his wife among the blessed, and celebrates their feast yearly on July 25. (*Wickipedia*)
3. Mark 15:10.
4. Adrian van Kamm, *Envy and Originality,* 1974, after Helmut Schoeck, *Der Neid: Eine Theorie der Gesellschaft,* 1966 (*Envy: A Theory of Social Behavior,* 1969) popularized in ten languages.

VII. PAUL'S AUTHORITY

1. George McCauley SJ, *The Truce of God,* (Denville: Dimension, 1972); *The God of the Group,* (Niles: Argus, 1975).

A. WHO IS PAUL?

1. Thiessen, *Jesus and the Forces of Death.* (2020).
2. Thiessen, *Contesting Conversion* (2011); *Paul and the Gentile Problem* (2016). See below, p. 111.

B. FOR WHOM DOES PAUL WRITE?

1. Thiessen, *Paul and the Gentile Problem*, pp. 44-46. Thiessen favors a readership of gentiles who have had themselves circumcised, as Paul taught his Galatian converts not to do. Historians since Stendahl label those "Judaizers." From Paul's rhetoric I argue here for lifelong Jewish readers instead.
2. For example, 1 Corinthians 1; Galatians 2:11, 3:1.
3. 1 Corinthians 9:24-27; Galatians 2:2; 2 Timothy 2:5, 4:7-8. Michael B Poliakoff, *Combat Sports in the Ancient World: Competition, Violence and Culture* (1987).
4. Hebrews 6:15, 11:33. Ephesians 6:12.
5. Genesis 30:8, 32:24.
6. Michael B Poliakoff, Chapter VIII "Metaphor, Myth and Reality," *Combat Sports in the Ancient World: Competition, Violence and Culture* (1987).
7. Ramsay MacMullen, *The Second Church: Popular Christianity A.D. 200-400* (2009).
8. Close paraphrase inserted at Exodus 32:12-14; 34:6-7. Numbers 14:18; 15:11. Stamped atop older threats of endless punishment at Exodus 20:6; Deuteronomy 5:10-12; 7:9-10. Numerous occurrences in Psalms and prophets.
9. Amos 1-3 // Romans 1-3.
10. Romans 2:28-29 cites Jeremiah 9:24-25 (Septuagint), problematic for Jeremiah's commentators. Thiessen, *Paul and the Gentile Problem*, pp. 68-70.
11. *Una Cosa Rara* by Vicente Martín y Soler (1786), played and named aloud in Mozart's *Don Giovanni*, Act II finale (Prague 1786).

C. HIS TRUE TRANSFORMATION

1. Acts 9.
2. Tobit 10, LXX. Wikipedia,"Cataracts," cites Cornelius Celsus (c. 25 BCE – c. 50 CE) *De Medicina*. See Dacher Keltner, *Awe* (2023), ch. 9.
3. See 1 Thessalonians 5:5; 2 Corinthians 4:6, 6:14; Philippians 2:15; Romans 2:19, 13:12. (See also the later attributed letters Colossians 1:12; Ephesians 5:8,13; 1 Peter 2:9, 2 Peter 1:19; 1 Timothy 6:16.)

D. HOW WORDS MATTER

1. Confucius, *Analects* 13:3.
2. Genesis 2:20-21.
3. Genesis 12, 17.
4. Genesis 12:1, Exodus 3:4.

VIII. HOW PAUL ARGUES IN ROMANS

1. Philippians 3:4-6.
2. Roman Catholic historians Nodet and Taylor winnow the gospel texts outside that Jordan story, concluding that Jesus and John Baptist never actually met. E. Nodet & J. Taylor, *The Origins of Christianity*, (1998), ch. ii.
3. Rick Fabian, *Signs of Life: Worship for a Just and Loving People*, (2019), pp. 63-65, links Byzantine mosaics at Palermo and coeval paintings from Florence.

A. A REVOLUTIONARY APPROACH

1. Romans 3.2.
2. Arthur Darby Nock, *Conversion: The Old and the New in Religion from Alexander the Great to Augustine of Hippo* (1933).
3. Matthew Thiessen, *Contesting Conversion: Genealogy, Circumcision and Identity in Ancient Judaism and Christianity* (2011), p.63.
4. Thiessen explores this metaphor extensively in *Paul and the Gentile Problem*, Part 2.
5. Though Hebrews is traditionally attributed to Paul, modern biblical scholars consider it to be written in the style of Paul by an unknown author.
6. Matthew Thiessen, *Paul and the Gentile Problem*, p. 67; also p. 59 following Origen.
7. 2 Cor. 12:4. Romans 8:26.
8. Kleinknecht in G. Kittel & G. Friedrich, *Theological Dictionary of the New Testament* (1964-1976,) iv, p. 77.

B. A COMMON PUZZLE: BIBLE LOGIC

1. Examples listed above in the following footnotes: Part 6, F.2; Part 7, B.8; Part 8, E.8.
2. Genesis 18.
3. Exodus 32. The historical event occurred under Israel's King Jeroboam I (1 Kings 12, 970 BCE) and was woven into the Mosaic story thereafter. See Note 6, above.
4. Ecclesiasticus 45:4. Hauck et al. in G. Friedrich, *TWNT,* (1968) vol. VI.
5. 2 Samuel 19:23, 1 Kings 17:18, John 2:4, even Matthew 27:4.

C. ANOTHER COMMON PUZZLE: PAUL'S LOGIC

1. Donald S. Prudlo, *Thomas Aquinas: A Historical, Theological, and Environmental Portrait,* (2020), ch. 3 and 6.
2. Illustration by W!B, *public domain via Wikipedia.*
3. (*mê génoito*), Romans 3:4,6,31. 6:2,15. 7:7,13. 9:14. 11:1,11. See Appendix 3.
4. Romans 3:1-2.

D. A THIRD COMMON PUZZLE: PAUL'S OTHER HEAD

1. Galatians 5:12 shows his usual fighting style in an uppercut punch.
2. 1 Corinthians 9:24-27; Galatians 2:2; 2 Timothy 2:5, 4:7-8.
3. Galatians 3:27-28. In Christ no Jew nor Greek.

E. A FOURTH COMMON PUZZLE: THE HUMAN ANIMAL

1. Philip Birnbaum, *A Book of Jewish Concepts* (1975), pp. 271-272, 658, cites *Genesis Rabbah 9:9.*
2. Roughgarden, Joan, *Evolution's Rainbow: Diversity, Gender and Sexuality in Nature and People* (2004). Robert Sapolsky and Michael Goldstrom, "The evolution of behavior," *Behave: The Biology of Humans at Our Best and Worst* (2017), ch.10.
3. Psalm 49:12, 20. Romans 8:6.
4. Romans 1:18-32.
5. Romans 1:32
6. Romans 2:1-4.
7. Romans 2:4.
8. Paraphrase inserted at Exodus 32:12-14; 34:6-7. Numbers 14:18; 15:11. Stamped atop older warning of endless punishment at Exodus 20:6. Deuteronomy 5;10-12; 7:9-10. Numerous references in Psalms and other prophets.
9. Luke 18:10-14.
10. Matthew 5:45. See Romans 2:11, 3:21.

F. OUR RELIGIOUS "NEEDS"

1. Genesis 3:9-13.
2. Peter L. Berger, *The Sacred Canopy: Elements of a Sociological Theory of Religion* (1967)
3. Collins, Francis S. *The Language of God: A Scientist Presents Evidence for Belief* (2006).

IX. PAUL'S FRIENDLY GOD

1. Romans 4:10-25. See also the timetable in Galatians 3 and the discussion of this in the chapter VI.A, above, "A Revolutionary Approach."
2. Romans 4:25
3. Romans 3:3, 22-26.
4. Genesis 2:15-25; Exodus 33:11.
5. Romans 7:12
6. Romans 1:21.
7. Romans 7:12.
8. Romans 7:7.
9. Romans 3:20.

A. WHAT IS SIN?

1. Romans 7:7.
2. Gen. 1:26.
3. See chapter 6.A, "Group Life: Tavistock."
4. Romans 7:7 Covert motives are parodied thus by George MacCauley SJ, *The Truce of God* (1972).
5. Genesis 3:9.
6. Stanley A. Leavy, *In the Image of God: a Psychoanalyst's View,* (1988), p.54.
7. Francis Bacon, "Of Truth," *Essays,* 1625.
8. John 18:34, 37. Zeki Saritoprak, "Who is Jesus for Muslims?" *The Christian Century,* June 2, 2017, pp. 32-34.
9. Romans 7:7.
10. Genesis 4:7; Psalm 10:9.
11. Romans 7:15-17.
12. Leavy, *In the Image of God,* p.65.
13. Romans 6:2, 7:13
14. Romans 11:29-32.
15. Romans 4:3, citing Genesis 15:6.
16. Romans 4:17.
17. Romans 5:20, 6:23. Houdini simile by George MacCauley SJ.
18. Romans 6:16.

19. Romans 7:24.
20. Romans 3:3, 22-26; 4:3.

B. GOD'S FREEDOM

1. Romans 2. Summary by George MacCauley, SJ, in *The Truce of God* (1972) and regular lectures at Fordham University and the University of San Francisco.
2. Romans 7:12.
3. Romans 3:6.
4. Romans 6:2,15.
5. Romans 9:14.
6. Thiessen, *Jesus and the Forces of Death*, pp. 177-185.

C. GOD'S ANSWER TO SIN

1. George MacCauley SJ in regular lectures at Fordham University and the University of San Francisco.
2. Galatians 3:13. Ref. Deuteronomy 21:23.
3. Romans 3:25.
4. Romans 3:3, 22-26.
5. Romans 5:6.
6. McCauley, *The Truce of God,* (1972); *The God of the Group,* (1975).
7. Romans 6:3-4.
8. Romans 11:1-11.
9. Leavy, pp 55-56.
10. Romans 8:5.
11. Leavy, p.56.

D. PRAYER THAT WORKS

1. Romans 8:2, 26-27. McCauley, *The Truce of God,* (1972).
2. Romans 8:14.
3. Romans 8:19.

E. GET A GUN

1. Romans 2:11, 3:21. See also James 1:16.
2. Romans 8:26.
3. 2 Corinthians 12:4.
4. Romans 8:2, 26-27.

5. Augustine, *Confessions,* Book I.

F. JOINED IN FUTURE

1. Romans 11:23-24.
2. 2 Corinthians 12:2.
3. Confucius *Analects* 13:3, trans James Ware, 1980. See full quotation on pg.115, above.
4. 1 Corinthians 13.
5. Simon May, *Love: a New Understanding of an Ancient Emotion,* (2019), Part 4.
6. 1 Corinthians 7:5-9.
7. Philosophers include A.J.Ayer, Bertrand Russell, Gerald Moore, A.N. Whitehead, and their Cambridge pupil Ludwig Wittgenstein.
8. RSV Editor R. Dentan finds no morally noble sense of *agapê* in secular Greek usage before the fourth century. See discussion on pp. 6-7 above and footnote 4.
9. 1 Corinthians 13.13.

X. FRIENDSHIP FOLDS IT ALL TOGETHER

1. John 15:13.
2. Nicholas A. Christakis, "Friends and Networks," *Blueprint: The Evolutionary Origins of a Good Society,* New York: Little, Brown Spark (2019).
3. Genesis 3:1-9.
4. Exodus 33:16.
5. Brian Hare & Vanessa Woods, "Survival of the Friendliest," *Scientific American*, August 2020, p.58.
6. Patience A. Schell, *The Sociable Sciences: Darwin and his Contemporaries in Chile* (2013), p. 6-7.
7. Robert Sapolsky, *Behave,* ch.14.
8. Some whales and birds can imitate a human melody but cannot modulate pitch or rhythm as all human cultures do, and they can sound simultaneously but not construct a harmonious chorus. Gary Tomlinson, *A Million Years of Music:* New York: Zone (2015), ch. ii., iv.
9. See interviews by musicians Helene Zindarsian and Jacob Slichter in Rick Fabian, *Signs of Life: Worship for a Just and Loving People,* (2019), ch. 10.

Made in the USA
Middletown, DE
16 September 2023